AF254405

-Gray Matter Press-

Summerland, B.C. Canada

1st - Edition

Paperback ISBN: 978-1-7771491-0-9

Ebook ISBN: 978-1-7771491-1-6

Printed by Kindle Direct Publishing/Amazon

All Scripture quotations, unless otherwise indicated are taken from the Holy Bible, New American Standard Version.

Book design & illustrations by Dustin Heigh

Edited by Brenda Timmer & Dianne Holland

MAGPIES, MOTORCYCLES, & MUKLUKS

CURIOUS TALES OF ADVENTURE AND GRACE

VOL. I

BEDTIME OR ANYTIME STORIES

FROM GRANDPA DEL

By: Del Riemer

Dedicated to my valued and much loved

Grand Children:

Danai

Kasey

Indianna

Jada

Mickey

Teagan

TABLE OF CONTENTS

Preface by Del Riemer 08

1. The Accident 13

2. The Snoopy 19

3. Just Moss 25

4. Timber 31

5. The Shower 37

6. Snake in a Jar 43

7. Rude Awakening 49

8. The Waterfall Reward 57

9. The Train 65

10. Buried Treasure 71

11. Stoned 81

12. Cut Throat 93

13. Christmas Lessons I - From the Wish Book 105

14. Christmas Lessons II - The Moccasins 113

15. He Dropped it Right in my Lap 121

16. The Parking Spot 129

17. Gus for Lunch 137

18. Bear in the Yard 149

19. Be Sure Your Sins Will Find You Out 159

20. My Dream Car 169

21. The Lemon 177

22. Beetle Board 187

23. Birds in the Chimney 193

24. Bromley Rock 199

25. The Magpie 209

PREFACE

Story - definition: *A narration of an incident or series of events in the life of a person, designed to interest or instruct the hearer.*

The book you hold in your hands is a collection of true stories from my life. These stories give life to my mistakes, failures and shortcomings which God has used to teach me lessons that are worth passing on. I think, most often, Grandparents tend to tell their children and grandchildren of all their successes, achievements and celebrations rather than admit to being weak, defeated or foolish. This tendency gives the impression that as we lived our lives, we did not make mistakes, and it actually sets us apart from the realities which our children and grandchildren experience daily. By sharing our failures and foibles, we communicate that we were no different from them, and that God in His patient grace and forgiveness can use even those times of weakness to teach lessons that can serve us for a lifetime.

In Joshua 4:20-24, we read how God had the heads of each Israelite tribe pick 12 large memorial stones from the Jordan river, and set them up at Gilgal as a reminder to the coming generations of all that God had done. Verse 24 says: "that all the peoples of the earth may know that the hand of the Lord is mighty, so that you may fear the Lord your God forever." Psalm 78: 5-7 says: "He commanded our fathers, that they should teach them to their children, that the generation to come might know, even the children yet to be born, that they may arise and tell them to their children, that they should put their confidence in God, and not forget the works of God, but keep His commandments..."

This book is a collection of my own 'Memorial Stones', intended to be read and reread by my children, grandchildren, great grandchildren... on down the line. These stories showcase the faithfulness, grace and reality of God in my life and the promise that He will do the same in the lives of all who read these words and surrender their own lives into His loving hand.

As you read these stories, I encourage you to consider similar times in your own life when God met you in powerful, unique or forgiving ways. Perhaps you might also want to record your own experiences to be passed on down as 'Memorial Stones' to those who come after you.

And to my own Grandchildren, I love you more than you will ever know, and God loves you even more than that! Please know that even though you will make mistakes throughout your life, God can turn them into lessons that will help you to grow into the very special people He has made you to be.

Enjoy these stories and pass them on!

All my love,

Grandpa Del

THE ACCIDENT

I was five years old and loved nothing better than to play in the neighborhood with my best friend Wayne. Wayne was a year younger than I was, and we were inseparable. Together we rode our bikes down the narrow, steep trails into the valley by the Highlands golf course, played football pretending we were the Edmonton Eskimos, and bravely skateboarded down our family's sloped driveway. One time when our street had just been paved, we took advantage of the smooth black asphalt and, with rocks and toys, created a super slalom course for our home-made boards. We practiced precarious turns, carefully following the course, raced around the home-made obstacles and gained speed by riding from the top of what seemed to be our mountain-high driveway. We filled many happy hours on that fresh black-top in front of our houses.

One day, preparing to skateboard down the driveway, I opened our garage door to get my board out. The garage door was an old, heavy, wood, one-piece door which had a large silver-coloured spring attached at the top. This spring helped to support the weight of the door when lifting it up and also brought the door down quickly and easily when closing. On the bottom edge was a heavy metal 'lip' which helped to protect the door as it clattered down to the paved driveway. This metal piece stuck out from the bottom of the door and offered an easy handle to grab. I had raised the garage door, gotten the skateboard out then yanked the door downward, thinking that Wayne was behind me on the driveway. The door barrelled down really fast and crashed into Wayne's head, slamming him with the hard piece of metal. The sound of that door striking Wayne's head was sickening. He screamed in pain and grasped his head in his hands, as a growing spot of blood soaked through his corduroy hat and dribbled down his face. Wailing at the top of his lungs, he raced for home.

I was terrified, heartbroken, and feeling very guilty for what I had done to my best friend. Would he die of this terrible injury? Would he be mad at me for the rest of his life? Would his mom call the police and have me arrested? I wept uncontrollably, not knowing what to do. I was so scared of what could happen that I hid in the corner of our garage where my dad kept a large pile of old newspapers. The pile was behind our bikes, the wheel barrow, and the lawnmower. I wedged myself deep into the corner, pulling a whole bunch of newspapers over me so that no one would be able to find me. I sat there for a long time, shivering and crying and thinking of what I might have to face for hurting my friend. I thought about what was happening to Wayne. Was he in the hospital, being taken there by an ambulance, having his head operated on? Did his parents hate me? Were the police on their way to find me? I don't know how long I crouched under the papers, but it was likely two hours or more. After what seemed to be a very long time, I heard the door of the garage open and someone came in. I heard my mother's voice call me, but I didn't answer. My mom looked around the garage for a long while before I felt the weight of the newspapers lift off my head and body. She reached down and lifted me into her arms, holding me for a long time as I, sobbing, tried to tell her what had happened. She gently explained that Wayne's mom had called on the telephone and said that Wayne had been hurt by the garage door at our place and that he had cut his head. It looked very serious because of the blood, but the doctor had said it was not a serious injury, just a fairly deep cut on his head. A few stitches had closed the wound, and once healed he would be fine. Wayne's mom said that I might be scared and sad and that I might even be hiding in a corner of the garage. Sure enough, she was right. Once mother found me, she assured me it was an accident and that, although I should have been more careful, it was not my fault. After a good cry and some milk and cookies, I felt better and looked forward to seeing Wayne and playing with him again. I was scared he might be mad at me when I saw him the next day but it was as though nothing had even happened. We played and skateboarded down the driveway like we always had, and never ever spoke about the accident again.

God sees and knows all the mistakes we make - the ones we do on purpose, and the ones we do by accident. Sometimes we feel bad and guilty, and sometimes we even 'hide' from the truth, thinking that maybe no one knows. God sees it all, but He loves us so much that He looks for us, finds us, and holds us close. The best thing we can do is to tell him of our failures and then thank Him for loving and forgiving us. Mistakes and failures are hard to accept, but if we are honest and admit them, God restores us and uses those mistakes to teach us lessons which make us better people.

Prayer: *God, thank you for loving us so much and for paying the price for our sins on the cross so that we can be forgiven and live free of guilt and regret. Give us soft hearts to learn from our mistakes so we can be the people who bring you pleasure. Amen.*

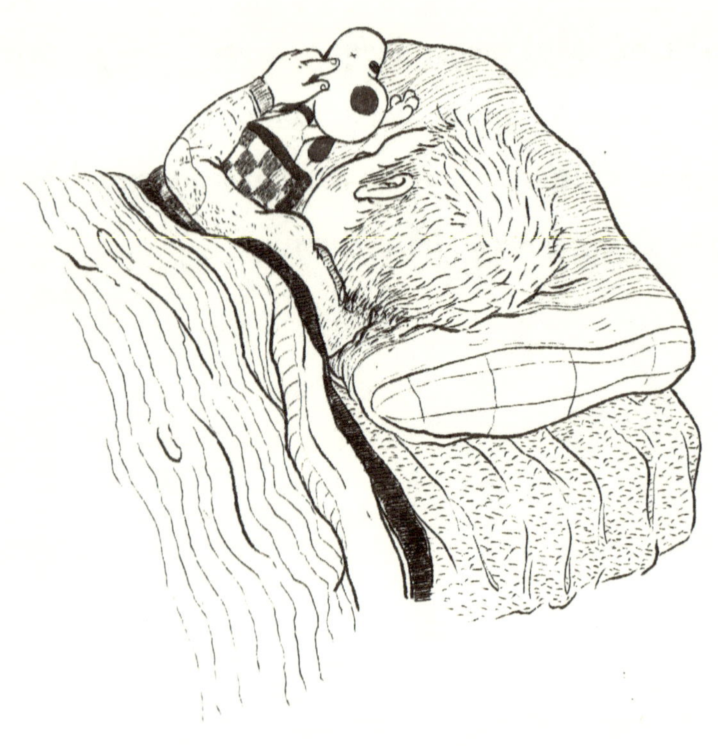

THE SNOOPY

Many years ago, my wife and I lived in a small town and worked with teenagers who were in trouble with the law. We partnered with several other couples and families to carry on this valuable ministry. Since we encountered difficult youth, we had to give serious consideration as to how we would discipline and lead our own children to good behavior and character. One of the other families on our staff team had a unique way of correcting their kids. I remember one time when their four-year old son was misbehaving, and some correction needed to be done. His mother sat the boy down and said to him, "Jesse, you have been acting very poorly and you need to do something about it, because if this behavior continues, I am going to take away your birthday and you'll be four forever!" Jesse's eyes glistened with tears as he wailed, "No Mom, I'll be good, please don't take away my birthday. I want to be five!"

Another story about this same family was the result of

damage to a stuffed animal. The young family loved God and brought Him into all aspects of their family activities. They attended church, prayed to God telling Him of their joys, sorrows and questions, and asked for His help when they were struggling. When someone was sick or going through difficulty, they would sit as a family and ask God for healing or wisdom in solving the situation. The family was always careful to praise and thank God for His goodness, not to just ask for things when they wanted something. When they prayed, they often used the word 'Hallelujah' which is a high form of thanks and praise to God. They would say: "Hallelujah Jesus. Hallelujah Jesus, thank you for your goodness." Jesse carefully watched and learned from his parents that God cares and is interested in what concerns us, that thankfulness is an important part of living for God.

Jesse had a stuffed 'Snoopy Dog', like the one in the Charlie Brown cartoons. It was his best buddy. He took Snoopy Dog wherever he went and even closely snuggled with Snoopy each night in bed. One day one of Snoopy's button eyes came off, so Jesse did what he had often watched his Mom and Dad do. He prayed...

"Howdedodah Deedus. Howdedodah Deedus. Heew da Snoopy, heew da Snoopy." His mother, opening the door a crack, heard little Jesse praying these words over and over while holding one hand in the air to seek God's favour, his other hand held over the missing eye on the face of Snoopy Dog. Soon Jesse was sound asleep with Snoopy Dog in his arms and the eye-button lying on the bedside table. Once Jesse was fast asleep, his mother quietly crept into the room, gently took the Snoopy from under Jesse's arm and picked up the loose button off the table. She sewed the eye firmly back on Snoopy Dog and placed it back in bed under Jesse's arm. The next morning she was awakened by loud praying coming from Jesse's room: "Howdedodah Deedus, you hewed da Snoopy, you hewed da Snoopy!" Jesse was acknowledging that his prayer had been answered and he wanted to give thanks to God for this miraculous healing!

Now, you might think that God didn't really do anything, it was Jesse's mother who had fixed the eye on Snoopy Dog; but actually, God wants to use us to be His hands and feet here on earth. When we pray for someone else, we need to let God know that we are willing for Him to use us to answer that prayer. Matt 5:16 says. "Let your light shine before men in such a way that they may see your good works, and glorify your Father who is in heaven."

Prayer: *Thank You, Jesus, that You hear every prayer we pray. Please use us to love the people around us and help us to be the people You want us to be. Amen.*

JUST MOSS

For roughly twenty years of my life, I worked as a certified climbing instructor and wilderness skills guide. This role gave me amazing opportunities to climb mountain peaks, experience scenic backpacking routes and ocean kayaking locations in the West Coast Gulf Islands, explore cave networks, surf beaches, bungee jump from high bridges and traverse wild back country ski routes. I had to maintain training and certification constantly to ensure that I would not lead others into dangerous situations.

As staff at a Bible College, I took a group of twelve leadership students to a chimney climbing site I used to teach on but had not revisited in a long time. (My kids used to 'chimney' up door jams by placing their back on one wall, while wedging their feet on the opposite wall and 'shimmying' up to the top of that door jam.) Over years, the landscape had changed. Trees and vegetation had grown into the chimney, sand and mud had filled in cracks, and anchors and man-made permanent protection had deteriorated. To get to the main part of the 'chimney' I had to guide my students through a series of rock outcrops and obstacles. One such obstacle, called 'The Vault', was a narrow fracture in the rock which was about 20 feet long but only about 16 inches wide. Climbers had to wedge themselves in between two opposing walls and slowly wiggle, with both front and back rubbing and scraping the rock. Wearing a slim backpack or even just a thick jacket made it impossible for a person to fit. In fact, when going through this narrow passage, even our climbing helmets would scrape along both sides of the wall. Once inside, we just had to squeeze, shimmy and wiggle slowly forward. As the instructor, when I got to the 'Vault', I shone my flashlight ahead to make sure there were no obstacles in the way and found, other than a tennis-ball-sized clump of moss that appeared to have grown out from a crack in the rock, the route looked clear. I took off my back pack with all our ropes, carabiners, water, and First Aid kit, and lashed it tightly to my leg so that as I wrestled my way through the vault, the pack would drag along behind me. I squeezed my way into the darkness while the rest of our group anxiously waited for me to make my way safely through before they would proceed one at a time.

Scraping my body through the vault, the pack dragging behind my trailing leg, my helmet roughly scraped both walls and I had to carefully shift my head to a different angle in order to squeeze through. About twelve feet into this narrow passage way, I was faced with the piece of moss I had noticed earlier. The moss, immediately in front of me, was such that I couldn't move my head to avoid it. I thought that as my helmet touched it, the clump would scrape off the wall and fall onto the floor of the passageway. My helmet made contact with the moss. Right in front of my eyes it moved. That's when I realized it was not moss at all! Two tiny black eyes opened as broad wings spread out from the furry body of a 'bat'! Its' mouth opened wide and I could see it's toothy fangs as the creature screeched in fright. I can't remember if I made the same sound as the bat or not, but I do know that I was just as startled as he was. Because I was so tightly wedged into the narrow space and barely able to move, it was a struggle to release my arm and sweep the little creature away from my face, dislodging it from the rock wall. Fortunately, I did not seem to harm the little guy. He shook his wings and flew out of the vault. Regaining composure, I slowly shimmied forward and in a few moments, extracted my body from the vault, relieved to be out safe and sound. I was then able to guide the others through a truly challenging adventure, but the bat was a reminder for me to assume nothing and always be prepared for the unexpected.

Sometimes in life we assume that something is harmless and no threat to us, but when we get closer, we realize that it is not what was expected, and we have to take action to avoid it. This is why we need God's guidance and the direction which comes from knowing Him and ask Him to lead us through life day by day. Life is full of exciting adventures, but it also has many unexpected obstacles to be avoided to keep us safe and on the right track. The Bible talks about Jesus being a 'Good Shepherd' who leads his sheep (us) to where we need to go. We must be careful to not run ahead or think that we know a better way. Let's trust Him and follow where He leads.

Prayer: *Lord Jesus, thank You for going with us through the journey of life, and guiding our steps to help us avoid the things and places You know may harm us. Thank You for loving us so much! Amen.*

JUST MOSS

TIMBER

A grocery store in our town draws many locals there to shop. It stocks vegetables and produce, meat and dairy items, frozen and canned goods, a bakery, and lots of pop, chips and candy. The manager often creates interesting displays showcasing items that are featured or are on sale.

One day I couldn't help but notice a large, stacked pyramid of Heinz Ketchup bottles. A seven or eight-foot-high 'mountain' of the glass bottles was stacked neatly from a square base of about four by four feet, to one single Ketchup bottle perched way up on top. It looked like a big Red Ketchup Christmas tree!

While shopping, I noticed a very loud and annoying 'beep, beep, beep', sometimes close by and sometimes several aisles away. I wondered what was making the noise until I turned a corner and saw an old, disabled man driving an electric shopping cart designed for handicapped persons. The cart was controlled by a 'joystick' which the man pushed to the left to turn left, right to turn right, and the further ahead he pushed the joystick, the faster his electric cart would move. He seemed to be travelling pretty fast and each time someone was in his way, he would push the horn button which let out a loud, obnoxious, honking screech. Most people who drive motorized carts are careful not to bump into those around them and usually slow down or stop if someone is not aware that they are there. This driver didn't seem to care. He rammed his way through the shoppers wherever he wanted to go and blasted his nasty horn every time someone got in his way. He even bumped right into an elderly lady without stopping or saying he was sorry. The old man's face, hardened into a scowl, looked really angry or just plain-old grumpy. I couldn't help but wonder why he seemed so bitter and uncaring. The basket attached to the front of the cart was empty, which raised the question in my mind whether he had any intention of buying anything or if he just wanted to annoy people. The honking continued throughout the store and I tried to keep my distance so as not to become one of his victims. I was kind of afraid of that man and the angry look on his face.

Just as I rounded the end of one of the grocery aisles, I

observed the electric cart heading for the Ketchup display. The passageway was a bit tight but there was still plenty of room for him to work the cart around the Ketchup pyramid. It appeared he had no such intention of avoiding the display. The cart didn't hit the Pyramid head on but glanced through the bottom row of the display, knocked out several bottles from the base which started an avalanche! I watched in horror as this massive seven-foot-high mountain of glass Ketchup bottles tilted precariously, then crashed to the floor in a splintering of glass and a massive splattering of bright red ketchup. What a mighty mess! The crash echoed throughout the grocery store as customers and staff looked on in horror. The guilty man's cart raced out through the automatic, sliding doors as fast as it would go. The driver didn't stop to see the mess he had created, nor did he offer any apologies. I wondered if he had done this on purpose.

Then, I watched as an amazing response to this accident took place. Staff started to direct customers around the disaster area while a cashier called over the intercom "Clean up on Aisle 4. Clean up on Aisle 4." I saw the boss, the store manager, make his way down the aisle carrying a mop, a bucket, a broom and a garbage can. I expected he would tell one of his staff to get busy and clean up the mess, but he didn't, he did it himself! Other staff offered their help, but the manager assured them that he had it under control and that they could continue serving the customers. What a great example he was!

I learned several lessons from observing the events that day. First, I realized that there are many people who have gone through difficult times and may be angry, bitter, lonely or sad. Perhaps if I had stopped to talk to the cart-driving man or asked if I could assist him in some way, or even just listened to his story, it would have changed all that happened. Second, it reminded me to observe people and not jump to conclusions about them, but rather to be available for God to use me to encourage or offer help in some way. Third, I learned from that store manager how to lead people when there are difficult things to deal with. This gracious manager handled the worst, dirtiest job himself with humour, grace, and without complaint. Because of his fine leadership, the rest of the employees were free to handle their tasks and look after the customers. I learned that to be a good leader, I need to set an example of what is right, to be forgiving and not judgmental.

The Bible reminds us that 'The Lord is slow to anger, abounding in love and forgiveness." Num. 14:18 Even Jesus, speaking from the cross, said "Father forgive them for they don't realize what they are doing." Luke 23:34 Let's treat people with love and respect and learn to lead by being a good example.

Prayer: *Jesus, Thank You for loving us even when we do wrong things. Give us patience and kindness by Your Spirit, so that others will see Your life in us and be drawn to you. Amen.*

THE SHOWER

As a wilderness trip guide, kayaking was my favorite way to travel around wilderness areas. A kayak keeps you close to the water, is stable and easily propelled. The tandem kayaks I used for guiding could have two paddlers on board, each in their own cockpit or compartment which was sealed from the ocean waves with a waterproof 'spray skirt'. Once a paddler is seated in the kayak, the skirt is stretched around the cockpit opening to seal the water out. With the spray skirt securely fastened, a kayaker can actually roll his boat upside down and back up again without taking on any water. This maneuver, called an 'Eskimo Roll', takes some practice, but it is a useful technique to learn to stay safe and dry in rough water.

Some of my favorite kayak trips were the three to four-day expeditions around B.C.'s West Coast Gulf Islands. We would see amazing sights: superb rock formations with shallow-water sea life like star fish, sea urchins, crabs, clams, small fish, coral shelves, barnacles and oysters. We would encounter seals, sea lions, otters, whales, salmon and eagles. As well as the variety of wildlife, we enjoyed seeing the beautiful and unique coastal homes and properties along the water's edge. It was a real pleasure to share these wonderful experiences with people who were unfamiliar with the West Coast ocean environment.

On one particular trip, my group of twelve, travelling in six tandem kayaks, paddled for three days and had camped at Blackberry point, Hole in the Wall, and Wallace Island. The weather had been perfect with warm temperatures and calm waters. Now we were heading back home to Thetis Island. The last day of the trip the winds were calm and it was very hot, causing us to sweat as we paddled across open water with home only a few hours away. Some complained of the heat and were wishing for a refreshing shower to cool them down.

In the distance we could see smoke rising from a forested area behind the town of Crofton where a pulp mill is located. Watching billowing plumes of smoke rise above the trees, we realized we were witnessing a forest fire! I could see a yellow water bomber scooping water from the ocean and flying over the fire to release its load. Heading across the bay, our kayaks out in open water, we seemed to be a long way from where the water bomber was flying low and scooping water. Then I noticed the pilot, flying in our direction, was dropping ever lower to reach water level. The sudden realization dawned that he was planning to do another scoop run with us directly in his path! The four powerful engines of the plane roared ever louder as he flew increasingly closer to our now-precarious position. Though a kayak is a nimble little vessel, it cannot just turn and move quickly out of the way of a fast-approaching water bomber. My first and most immediate thought was to contact the pilot on my marine radio. I calmly called on the emergency frequency. No answer! As the plane's belly touched the water and began to scoop, I calculated that our safest and best action was to gather all the kayaks into a small tight group rather than be too spread out. We quickly rafted up the six boats together. What if that fast-flying plane with its big bay doors wide open happened to scoop up a kayak or two and inadvertently drop them onto a raging forest fire?

All our eyes and ears focused on the four screaming engines

as they agonizingly laboured to lift the plane off the water again. It was heading right for us and there was nothing we could do about it! I prayed - fervently. If the pilot of that plane couldn't see us and didn't know we were there, God certainly did. He could intervene and get that plane into the air before it struck any of our kayaks. The plane sped closer and closer as the engines roared in an effort to increase speed and lift off. With only seconds to spare the plane began to rise, was finally above us and still climbing. As he roared noisily over our heads, a cool, refreshing shower of water from the bottom of the plane sprayed us all. The complaining kayak-paddler's wish was realized!

I was reminded that indeed God knows who we are and where we are at every moment, and He has plans for us that only He knows. All the kayakers on that trip will never forget that memorable experience and the way God met the desire of our hearts in a way we would never had expected. Life is like that! God will take us through things that we may not choose, but He loves us and desires the very best for us. He will teach us if we are willing to listen and respond.

Prayer: *Lord Jesus, thank You for walking with us through life, even in the middle of things that are frightening or confusing. Remind us to keep our minds, our trust and our hope in You alone. Oh, and thanks for giving us cool showers and meeting our needs, even in ways we don't expect! Amen.*

SNAKE IN A JAR

When my son Luke was young I would often take him along to help me teach rock climbing to guest groups who attended our conference center. Even at 10 years old Luke was fully trained and very good at belaying climbers and rappelers. (Belaying is when an instructor controls the safety rope attached to a climber.)

One hot summer day we had a teen youth group at our conference center. Luke and I taught a rappelling course. The participants would hike up a narrow pathway to a high plateau where they would wait their turn to get harnessed up and be securely attached to a rope. They would then lower themselves over a 60-foot cliff face. Upon reaching the bottom, they would disconnect themselves from the rope and trek the path to rejoin the group at the top of the cliff. Mid-afternoon, a couple of the youth told me they had heard a 'rattling' sound coming from underneath a large boulder they had passed while hiking back up the path. I suspected a rattlesnake was coiled up under the rock and I told the group to stay clear of the boulder to avoid aggravating the snake and potentially getting bitten. On completion of the course, I instructed the group to return to the bus and wait for Luke and me while we packed up the equipment.

Ropes and equipment secured, Luke and I checked out that large boulder to see if there actually was a rattlesnake hiding underneath. I picked up a stick long enough to enable me to poke deeply under the rock. As the stick disturbed the area, there was that unmistakable rattle confirming what we had suspected. I poked again to coax the snake out from its hiding place, being fully aware if I got too close it could strike. The rock was near the edge of the cliff we had been rappelling down and directly below was a large bush. I encouraged the snake to the edge of the cliff and carefully pushed it over where it fell harmlessly into the bush below. As Luke and I made our way back down the path, we searched for a forked stick. I found one that was about four feet long and had a perfect fork which could be used to pin the snake's head to the ground without hurting it. As the reptile slithered out of the bush, I deftly secured its head with the forked stick. Then, carefully grasping the snake immediately behind the fork, I picked it up while keeping firm hand pressure on the head to open and immobilize the jaws and fangs. Once the head was safely secured, Luke and I could clearly see the fangs and open mouth without any danger of being bitten. As I was holding the snake, it wrapped its angry flailing body around my arm while rattling its tail in warning. We boarded the bus with the rattler coiled around my arm and its mouth wide open. The youth on the bus froze, wide-eyed, in terror.

"Does anyone have a nylon windbreaker with a large zippered pocket?" I casually asked. Within moments the right style of jacket was volunteered. Luke opened the zipper and cautiously held it wide enough for me to deposit the snake inside. Uncoiling the frightened reptile from my arm, I placed its head deep inside the pocket and carefully removed my hand. Luke quickly closed the zipper, and together we deposited the jacket on the front seat of the bus. The teens watched nervously as the nylon jacket wriggled and twisted and shifted around on the front seat.

Arriving back at the Camp Lodge, I brought the jacket into

the main living room where all the youth campers were gathered. A huge, clear glass jar from the kitchen would make a good terrarium for the snake so we could observe it safely. Luke located a few rocks, a bit of grass and a couple of sticks and lowered them into the jar. I held the jacket over the jar, carefully opened the zipper, manipulated the snake into the jar, and screwed on the hole-punched lid which allowed the snake to freely breathe. The kids eagerly gathered around to see a close-up of the wild creature. Then, in my temporary absence, a couple of boys decided it would be fun to shake the glass jar and make the snake mad (probably in an effort to scare the girls). One boy picked up the jar and gave it a violent shake. The rocks rattled around in the glass jar and broke a large, single piece out of the side. The snake was angry, rattling, and heading for freedom out of the new escape hatch. Screaming in fear, the kids jumped way back. The foolish boy holding the jar let it drop onto the table in fear and horror. Luke, responding to the screams, ran into the room, quickly assessed the situation, grabbed the broken glass piece and held it firmly over the jar opening that the snake was slithering towards.

"Get my Dad!" Luke yelled. Immediately noting the

precarious predicament Luke was in, I quickly grabbed another large glass container and we safely transferred the rattler into it. Later, Luke and I found a better-sized aquarium, deposited the snake in its new home, and then took it to our home to raise as a pet.

Sometimes in life, we make mistakes with no intention of doing anything wrong; kind of like that teen that shook the jar just to get the snake excited. God understands our mistakes and He always provides a way for us to make things right and move on. Sometimes there are long term consequences to our mistakes, but it's what we choose to do about it that can allow us to mature and grow.

Prayer: *Father God, thank You for loving us even when we make mistakes and thank You for using those things to teach us. Draw us closer to listen and teach us to depend on You. Amen.*

RUDE AWAKENING

It was the summer of 1973, just after high school graduation, when my friend, Tom, talked me into going on a road trip to celebrate grad. Yellowstone National Park in rugged Wyoming beckoned us with a sense of great adventure.

Once Tom's Volkswagen Beetle was loaded with camping gear, food, a change of clothes, and a map of the United States, we set off with eager anticipation. We traveled through the wilderness, rugged mountains, and steep canyons of Wyoming; we talked about our plans for the future and where they would one day take us. Our wallets were pretty thin so we decided on the free campsites marked 'Primitive' on the Yellowstone map. There would be no paved roads, no restrooms with flush toilets and no showers. Water had to be drawn from the creek that meandered through the campground. There would be no picnic tables, and the campfire rings were just a circle of rocks. Even the road to the primitive sites was an adventure with dips, potholes and washouts making it difficult for any vehicle to get through. At one point, a creek had overflowed its banks carving a deep trench of mud and rock where the road had once been. The washout had created a sharp drop-off spanning the creek bed that was approximately eight feet across. There was no water in the trench at that time of year, but there were plenty of rocks and muddy spots to get us terribly stuck. We climbed out of the car to figure out how to navigate around (or over) the problem. Searching the surrounding area for anything useable, we stumbled across a couple of long planks and a heavy, wooden beam. We placed the planks and beam across the span of the trench then stood back to admire our fine makeshift bridge. We were not sure the beam would hold the weight of our little car, or if the width of the planks would be wide enough for our tires, but after all our hard work we had to try. Tom took the driver's seat of the VW and ever so carefully inched the vehicle onto the primitive home-made bridge while I yelled directions from the opposite bank. I painstakingly lined up the tires with the beam and planks, giving hand signals to keep Tom in the middle of the rickety bridge.

Slowly, slowly, the car hesitantly edged its way over the muddy trench below. The weathered-wood 'bridge' flexed and creaked and groaned under the weight of the Beetle. Tom and I unconsciously held our breath and our muscles tightened as we watched with tense anxiety. It held! With a sense of great engineering ingenuity, we made it to the other bank!

The campground was only a few hundred metres further down the trail and we chose a beautifully rugged spot near the rushing creek. That would be our water supply and washing station. We were the only people around, several miles from the nearest road, and that was just the way we wanted it. "What an adventure," we thought, "it doesn't get any better than this!"

We set up our two-man pup tent and quickly started a fire in the rock fire ring. Our scrumptious supper of macaroni and cheese with hot dogs roasted over the open fire made us feel like kings in our own private kingdom. The only sounds were the rushing of water in the nearby creek and the wind softly whispering through the trees. We sat and talked and laughed late into the wee hours of the night while stoking and poking at the campfire. Finally, exhausted, we crawled into our little tent for a good night's sleep.

Sometime in the early dawn, both of us were fitfully awakened by a strange, grunting sound. The tent was shaking, and with the morning sun shining low over the horizon, we could see the shadowy silhouette of a huge bear projected on wall of our tent. It would grunt and huff as though catching a whiff of a strong smell and then push its nose against the side of the tent, stretching the thin nylon fabric inward. The bear would then pull back and pace for a few seconds as if trying to figure out how to get at the appetizing aromas inside. Tom and I were terrified as we imagined what would happen if the bear took a swipe at the tent with its enormously long, sharp claws. We would be breakfast! I just wanted to crawl back into my sleeping bag, pull it over my head and pretend I was having a bad dream, but Tom had another idea. For some unknown reason, when we went to bed the night before, we had brought the hatchet into the tent with us. It being the only weapon we had, Tom decided that rather than waiting to be attacked, he would strike first. Anxiously perched on top of my sleeping bag, I watched and prayed that God would see us and save us.

Tom squatted on his sleeping bag, grasped the hatchet with both hands and waited for the bear to poke his nose against the tent again. After more pacing and grunting, the bear came close, pushed against the tent with his nose while taking long, deep, noisy snuffs. Tom raised the hatchet and forcefully slammed the blunt end down with all his might. The sound of the hatchet making contact with the bear's nose was a sickening combination of crunching and squashing as steel met tissue and bone! I will never forget the bear's angry bellowing as it raced, howling, far into the distance. The only other sound we heard was a garbage can being knocked over as he raced back into the forest. The sound of his bawling never really stopped until he was just too far away for us to hear it anymore.

Tom and I realized with mutual relief that we weren't going to die that morning after all. We joyfully high fived and crawled out of the tent into the cool morning air feeling strong and powerful. As we talked about what happened we realized that in our extreme fear and sense of helplessness, we had both individually prayed that God would save us. We took time to thank Him for His protection and for hearing the prayer of two terrified boys who had nowhere else to turn.

I learned that morning that life has many difficulties and tragedies, and often there is nothing we can do about them. It is comforting to realize that God sees us, knows us and promises to never leave or forsake us. Just as God shut the mouths of the lions when Daniel was thrown into their den, and as He guided the stone from David's sling to take down Goliath, all He asks is that we acknowledge Him and trust Him with our whole heart.

Prayer: *Lord Jesus, You said in Your Word that 'it's not by might nor by power but by Your Spirit' that victory is won. (Zech. 4:6) Let me trust You every moment, and not just as a last resort. Thank You for loving and caring for me ... and watching over me both when I'm awake, and when I'm asleep! Amen.*

55

THE WATERFALL REWARD

Every June, for many years, I have gone on a two-week motorcycle trip with a group of friends and relatives. We have traveled all around BC, and through many States in the US. Every trip has a destination, either in terms of a place we want to get to, or an event we plan to attend. We have ridden down the Oregon Coast highway with its beautiful ocean scenery, visited the geysers in Yellowstone National Park, camped in the California Redwoods, sailed on the Southern Gulf Island ferries from island to island, and attended Major League baseball games, NASCAR races, and outdoor musical concerts. On this particular trip, our goal was to find and enjoy as many natural 'hot springs' as possible. One of our group purchased a book that gave a description and location of 25 or 30 of them. We biked through the states of Montana, Wyoming, Idaho, Nevada, Oregon, and Washington, where many of the Hot Springs could be found. Some of these naturally-warm pools were spectacular; some were very difficult to reach.

The guidebook 'map' we used to direct us described one hot spring near a campground. The trail to that particular hot spring actually started in the campground, so it was decided that would be a good place to spend the night. Arriving late afternoon in fading daylight, we set up our tents, enjoyed a hot supper, then followed our guide book directions to the trail head. We began at the parking lot and descended downhill toward the Payette River, where the trail unexpectedly ended. Since it was June, the peak of the mountain snow melt, the river was a fast-flowing torrent of freezing, muddy, water. Somewhat confused, we stopped and pondered which direction to take. Referring back to the guidebook, we found we could wade into the river and hike upstream for approximately 200 yards, the length of two football fields!

The water was freezing cold and flowing so fast it was difficult to make any headway. Compounding the difficulty, the river bed was full of rocks causing us to stumble and back track before making any forward progress. Added to that, we were losing daylight as we fought the strong current. Suddenly we faced a steep canyon wall on our right. There appeared to be no way around this shear wall, and no way to get to shore to go around it. Our only option was to continue to follow the wall upstream, struggling against the current while hanging on to any crack or handhold in the face of the rock. The water, becoming progressively deeper, enveloped us chest deep in freezing water, threatening to sweep us off our feet and drag us down river. All shivering seven of us, lined up one behind the other and painstakingly inched our way along the canyon wall, grabbing at any handhold we could reach in order to stay on our feet. We were completely unaware that John, the fellow at the tail-end of the group, could not swim and was terrified of even being in the water! Barely clinging to the rock wall, John was quietly and courageously struggling to keep up with the rest of us. Even if John had yelled for help, the noise of the raging river was so loud we could not have heard his cries.

It seemed like a very long distance and an even longer time, before I finally rounded a bend in the river with the others following close behind. The canyon wall suddenly ended and a shallow shore line emerged. What a relief to finally stagger out of the freezing river and experience solid footing once again! As we stepped thankfully onto the shore I heard another water sound that was very different than the thunder of the thrashing river. About 40 feet up the side of the canyon wall, a cascading waterfall dropped like a curtain into a pool. It produced steam that billowed up like smoke from a campfire. A clear trail up the steep incline led us to an incredibly beautiful pool, about four feet deep and 20 feet long. This natural thermal pool was filled to overflowing from the hot spring waterfall cascading from above. After the frigid river-water experience, the welcome heat embraced us like a loving hug. We joined ourselves with other people sitting in this natural Jacuzzi, and we talked, laughed and related our exciting experience of the treacherous journey that brought us to this warm, natural 'wonder'. Knowing that to return to our campsite we would have to navigate the same frigid water, we lingered for perhaps an hour and a half in the comfort of God's creative 'hot tub'.

Eventually, we worked up the courage to once again navigate the frightening return adventure that carried fresh risks and difficulties. Now night time and completely dark, we were grateful that one of our group had thought to bring a headlamp which provided enough light to make our way back down the trail to the river. We stumbled step after uneasy step through the frigid water, as the ruthless downstream current attempted to drag us into its vicious clutches. Once again, we clung to almost invisible handholds in the canyon wall, struggling to reach the trail that would lead us to the parking lot and then our campsite. On this return journey John was in the middle of the group to ensure he would be safe and secure!

I'm sure you are imagining what that adventure must have been like. Perhaps you can almost feel the strong tug of the current, the freezing water, the relief of the hot waterfall, and then the terrifying hike back in the dark. You might wonder if it was 'worth it', or if we would ever try it again, given the opportunity. Well, I have to say that all the difficulties, risks, and discomfort made the destination that much more rewarding! I don't think the hot pool at the base of that waterfall would have been nearly as welcome, or as spectacular, if we hadn't just navigated the terrifying route that got us there. This reminds me of the difficulties of life. We all go through hard times and fearful experiences and sometimes just want to give up. But it is these things that draw us to call out to God for help, for safety, for assurance, and then He responds with His deep love and warm embrace. He knows who we are, where we are, and what we are going through, and He is just waiting for us to place our trust in Him. The older I get, the more I call out to Jesus, and the more I realize that He hears my voice and gives me everything I need. This is a good habit to practice. Make sure to include Jesus in all your plans and everything you do.

Prayer: *Lord Jesus, I know that even when I find myself in sad, scary or lonely places, You are with me. Thank You for making my life worthwhile and giving me Your warm embrace, like a hot waterfall on a cold dark night. I love you Jesus! Amen.*

63

THE TRAIN

One of the things I love about riding motorcycle is the time to get away from responsibilities and life's pressures, just to be 'alone in my helmet'! I have purposely never used a motorbike intercom to allow me to talk to other riders, just so I can think, pray, listen to music and experience 'rest' as I travel.

On one particular day I had traveled alone for a full day before meeting up with a group of friends waiting for me on the Oregon Coast, just south of Portland. I had a long ride ahead of me travelling into the United States, south through Washington State, and then west along the Washington-Oregon border to the Pacific Ocean.

At this particular time in my life, I was pastoring at Summerland Baptist Church and was responsible for the music, small groups, seniors, and outreach of that church. They were difficult times. I was feeling criticized, worn down and discouraged. I was filled with self-doubt and even doubting God. Did God really care, or even know my situation? Was He listening to my prayers? Did it matter to Him that I was feeling so low that I even wondered about giving up? Even though I had many reasons to hope and see God all around me, I was pretty well wrapped up in my own self-pity. I didn't even really want to listen to encouragement.

As I rode the scenic, almost deserted highway along the Columbia River that day, I pleaded, "God, I know that compared to You and this vast world You have made, I am just a speck of dust. If you really care and love me, prove it God, prove it!"

It was a straight stretch of the highway with railway tracks running parallel, and way up ahead I could see the caboose of a freight train. I was going faster than the train, gaining on it, and soon I was right across from the caboose. I passed the freight cars, tankers, flat beds with stacked-up shipping containers, grain cars loaded high and secured with tight strapping, and finally caught up to the black, smoke-belching locomotive as it strained to pull the heavily-loaded rail cars. The train was so close on my left that I could hear the rumble of its wheels and feel the vibration of the road beneath me. Just ahead was a bridge which allowed the highway to pass over the train tracks and the train to pass under the road and continue on the 'right' side of the highway. As the train passed under the highway, and I rode over the train on the bridge, I came alongside the main locomotive engine. I could see the engineer sitting by the open window, his left arm resting on the sill. I slowed down to match his speed so that the engineer and I were right next to each other. We seemed to be only about twenty feet apart because I could clearly see his hat, his moustache, his hairy arm and the whites of his eyes. It was a special moment of connection as I looked at him and he looked at me. We smiled at each other, me on my little touring motorcycle, and he in his powerful, long and mighty diesel locomotive. With an amused grin, I gave him a couple of quick beeps with my motorcycle horn, which actually sounds kind of like the 'beep-beep' from those roadrunner cartoons. The engineer responded with a mischievous grin, pulled his arm from the sill, then reached up and grabbed the cord of the trains' mighty air horn. Once activated, the air horn on top of that huge diesel engine, created a deep and awesome earsplitting roar that almost blew me off the road. He let the horn blow for maybe three seconds, let off for a moment, blew another short burst, and then a final burst for another full three to four seconds. I think he saw my bike swerve from my shock and surprise at the volume and magnitude of that blast. His head was bobbing up and down with laughter as he looked at me face to face. I laughed too and gave him a friendly nod as I increased my speed, leaving the slower-moving giant in the distance.

When that air horn blew, it was as though God had spoken directly to me; "Of course I exist, and while I am infinitely powerful and enormous, that doesn't mean that I don't care, or don't know what you are going through. Make no mistake, Del, I love you deeply and am with you through these difficult times. I will always be there for you. I want you to remember every time you hear a train whistle or horn, that you are loved, cared for and watched over by Me!"

With tears streaming down my face, I realized that God had just spoken directly to me in my lowest time. He really did know and love me. He would always be there for me. No matter how big or small my problems or concerns, He understood and would embrace me and walk with me. Even after many years, these thoughts still fill my mind whenever I hear a train whistle, air horn or even a motorcycle beep-beep!

Prayer: *Thank You so much Lord for reminding us every day that You love us and that we are not alone, no matter what comes our way! Oh, and God, let me listen carefully for Your voice so that I recognize it even when You speak in unusual ways. Amen.*

BURIED TREASURE

Riding my motorcycle - it's one of my favourite pastimes! I think everyone has something they love to do which brings them joy and gives them opportunity to spend time with others who enjoy the same thing. I didn't actually start riding motorcycles when I was a kid. In fact, I clearly remember at probably only 11 or 12 years old, I was at my cousins' farm where they had a small dirt bike. They showed me how to use the throttle to go faster, the brakes to slow down and the clutch to shift gears. It all seemed pretty simple, yet when I turned the throttle with my right hand, the bike quickly and unexpectedly jerked forward. Holding on as tightly as I could, my body was thrown back by the force of the acceleration, and my right hand involuntarily turned the throttle adding even greater speed. Desperately trying to figure out what to do, the bike sped toward the freshly-planted garden dead ahead. My attempts to turn were futile. I had no option other than to simply 'survive' this 'rocket' into outer space! I flew through the garden opening and straight into the soft soil, the tires digging deep into the tilled dirt. The bike slowed as small plants were either plowed under or spit out by the back tire. Hitting the fence at the end of the garden, I fell over, scared and embarrassed, but unhurt. I didn't ride a motorcycle again until I was in my late 20's.

Some years later, a friend asked if I wanted to go for a ride on his Yamaha Midnight Special 1000cc. I thought it would be fun, and safe seated on the back, with him driving. As we roared down the highway for about 15 kms, I truly enjoyed the speed, the feel of the wind in my face, the smells, and the wide-open views from the back of the bike. The driver pulled over on the side of the highway and climbed off. I thought perhaps he had to pee or something so I got off as well, waiting for the ride home. To my surprise and panic, he looked at me, and said, "Well Del, you are driving us back home!"

"I have never driven a big motorcycle before and besides, I don't have a license!" I gulped. I'm sure I looked stunned and tense.

"I'll talk you through it, and you'll love it. Besides, I'm not taking 'no' for an answer. If you want to get back home, you're going to have to drive the bike,' cause I'm not driving" he said firmly. Hesitantly, and with more than just a little fear, I straddled the bike and sat on the front seat. He got on the back and told me what to do. I was freaked out as this was a large, heavy machine with an adult passenger on the back. Under my friend's instruction, I let out the clutch a bit too quickly and the bike lurched forward, almost throwing us off. I managed to maintain control and shifted through the gears as he yelled step-by-step instructions into my ear. Within seconds we were speeding freely down the highway and my fear and hesitation turned to excitement and exhilaration. I clearly remember thinking as the wind blew through my hair that this was the most fun I had had in a long time and I needed to get me one of these motorcycle contraptions! Soon after that ride I bought a bike and have been riding ever since.

My greatest experiences on a motorcycle have been the trips with my two sons, Luke and Brad. I have taken each of them on a motorcycle camping trip every summer since they turned 5 years old. Our three to five-day trips took us all over BC and Alberta, and South into the U.S. We saw many amazing sights and spent loads of time fishing and exploring. Tent camping also meant cooking our meals on a little one-burner camping stove. After all those years and trips, I told the boys that once they were old enough, they could each get their own motorcycle license and I would buy a second bike for them to ride. Another bike would allow us to ride together on a longer trip down the Oregon Coast to California before they graduated from High School and left home. Both of the boys did exactly that and we each have an amazing trip etched in our memory. The trip that our oldest, Luke, and I took down that West Coast Highway holds many memories, but one in particular sticks in my mind.

It was raining heavily as we rode south down the Oregon Coast with the Pacific Ocean on our right and scenic landscapes, light houses, farms, and towns on our left. At the Oregon/California state line we came to a town called Brookings. We were wet and cold and it was lunch time. We pulled over at a small-town café to dry out, warm up and have something to eat. As we slid into a booth in the restaurant and started to remove our rain suits, a couple in their mid-40's, sitting at a table just across the aisle from us, called over and commented that we must be riding motorcycles. This was pretty obvious since we were dressed in rain gear and carrying helmets. They expressed interest in what kind of bikes we were riding. After telling the make and model of our motorcycles, I returned the question. "Considering your interest in our bikes, I assume you ride as well. What kind of bike do you folks ride?"

The lady smiled. Her husband was pretty quiet and seemed content to let her do the talking. "Well, we have a 1921 Indian motorcycle" she replied. Both Luke's and my eyes widened with amazement since that bike is one of the most classic, rare and valuable bikes in existence.

"Wow, how did you ever get hold of a bike like that?" I asked. "Did you find an old one and restore it?"

She replied: "No, actually it's brand new."

"Oh, it must be one of those replica bikes designed to look like an original," I responded.

"No, it is a brand new, original 1921 Indian motorcycle," she corrected me.

Luke and I were baffled. That bike was over 80 years old, how could it be brand new?

"How in the world do you have a brand new 1921 Indian?" I asked. She began her amazing story.

"My husband and I grew up here in this little town and had jobs that didn't pay very much money. We always wanted to buy a house and have a family, but we never seemed to have enough money to even make a down payment, so we rented for many years." She continued:

"Then, just a couple of years ago, we decided that since we were getting older, we needed to do whatever we could to purchase a home for ourselves. We looked at what was for sale and found a hundred-year-old house that needed a lot of fixing up. Maybe between a bank loan and what we had saved we could buy it. We went to the bank and borrowed as much money as possible, and although we now had a huge debt, at least we had a house of our own!"

The lady paused for a sip of coffee before continuing.

"After moving into the house," she went on, "we looked

around at how we could renovate and fix it up, but we just couldn't afford much. Downstairs we noticed a strange jog in the wall that appeared to be wasted space. Maybe if we tore that wall down, we could make the room bigger and use the materials to build another wall somewhere else in the house. Using hammers and crowbars we broke through the layers of plaster and wood and were soon looking at a tiny room containing a large wooden crate with another smaller wooden box on top of it. After digging our way through the chopped-up wall, we opened the small box and, to our amazement, found it full of all kinds of old jewellery; rings and broaches and necklaces. Thoroughly excited, we then worked at opening the large container. It was an original shipping crate for a brand new 1921 Indian Motorcycle! The bike was still greased up and in show room condition."

"No way!" Luke and I simultaneously exclaimed in wide-eyed amazement.

The woman paused, smiled and then picked up her story.

"Oh, it was amazing all right, but that isn't even the best part. We took the jewellery to a local jeweller and had the contents appraised. When the jewellery was sold, with the amount of money raised we were able to pay off the entire mortgage of the house! We were left with a totally debt free house and a brand new 1921 Indian Motorcycle."

The woman appeared a little sheepish as she told us they had known two families from town who had owned that house before she and her husband bought it. Both families had used the larger space as a recreation room, even had a recliner chair sitting within two feet of the treasure that would have changed their lives, but they didn't know it!

Wow, what a story, and what makes it even more amazing . . . it is true! Luke and I didn't just hear this story from TV or read about it in a book, we heard it from the very people who had experienced it!

I have thought about that story many, many times over the years, and thought how it is like so many people who live their whole lives just struggling to get by. They work, strive to build their lives, marry and have kids but never experience true freedom and joy. Yet, right close by, there is a treasure by the name of 'Jesus', who wants to forgive their sins and give life and hope and freedom. People are too busy to notice and have built walls to keep Him away, or they simply don't care. As a consequence they miss the amazing life He would give them. There just needs to be a willingness to tear down the walls that keep them from Jesus and allow Him to pay off the mortgage of their lives and set them free!

Luke and I will forever remember that motorcycle trip. More importantly, we will never forget the story of the 1921 Indian Motorcycle and the lesson it taught us.

Prayer: *Lord Jesus, thank You for loving me and for dying on the cross to pay off the sins and wrong things I have done. Thanks that I can have freedom and rest from all my fears, my mistakes, and my efforts to be good enough for You. Thank You that You will always be my treasure that is as close as my very breath! Amen.*

CHAPTER II

STONED

While kayaking through the Southern Gulf Islands of British Columbia, I have seen some magnificent sights and camped in some amazingly beautiful locations. One such place is on the west side of Valdez Island. I remember the first time I kayaked under the huge sandstone cliffs, intricately carved by thousands of years of wind and pounding waves, and chiseled by the sting of tiny pressured sprays of salt water. This time-produced, natural sculpting is like a work of art with a 'Dremel' tool done by a gifted artist. The huge walls have become a honeycomb of lace-like designs joined together with lines, colours, and spider webs of sandstone connecting each facet of the sculpture. The cliffs soar from about ten feet above sea level to nearly 200 feet high. Right at sea level is an amazing formation created by the rise and fall of the tide and the pounding waves over thousands of years. The lower edges of the cliffs are chiseled into a wave-shaped tunnel which, when the tide is just right, a kayaker can paddle through. This amazing undercut of the cliff wall sweeps up and over the kayaker, then curves back down to water level on the outside edge. I have guided many people who became speechless with awe, as they traversed this natural phenomenon.

One wonderful and unique natural cliff face became a rappel site for our summer programs. It has proven to be an exciting and adventure-filled site to offer guests who visit the conference facilities on Thetis Island.

Rappelling is a technique used for people to descend or move down a cliff face to the bottom. The instructor or cliff master secures one or two strong static-line ropes to a solid anchor point. Once the ropes are secured, they are thrown over the face of the cliff and hang there until needed for the down climb. One more rope, a safety line connected to the climber, is controlled independently by a belayer. The belayer keeps the belay rope snuggly attached to the rappeler and controls their rate of descent.

Before I set up the Valdez location to be used as a rappel site, I first needed to make sure it was safe for inexperienced guests. To check out the cliff, I secured my own ropes, rappelled down the face to ensure the rock was secure and that no rocks or other obstacles could come loose and strike a rappeler. I carried a broom with me to clean off the rock and sweep loose debris out of the cracks and off rock ledges. There was one fairly large rock ledge, about 15 feet down that would make a great place for the rappeler's first landing. From there they could get their bearings and launch themselves down the overhang part of the cliff. (An overhang is a rock formation which sticks out from the vertical cliff face and must be navigated around or over to descend the cliff.)

Once the site was checked out, cleaned up, and secured, I felt ready for groups of people to experience the excitement and adventure of rappelling! Since the cliff was located directly over the water I would need to ensure there was a boat sitting directly under the rappeler to prevent him from dropping into the ocean. He would land in the boat, untie the ropes, be escorted to a nearby landing area where he could then step ashore and follow the trail back to the top to await his turn to rappel again.

Over the next months, I brought dozens of people to that site and watched them enjoy the challenge and feel the amazement of rappelling in such a unique and spectacular location. On one trip the following summer, I took a group of ten youth, loaded into two separate boats, to make the 40-minute journey across the glassy waters of the Gulf Islands to our rappel site on Valdez Island. My son Luke was an assistant instructor for these courses, and his job on this day was to navigate the inflatable Zodiac boat underneath the rappeler as he neared the bottom of the cliff face. My youngest son, Brad, was part of the group of youth who would rappel down the cliff. He was 13 years old and had some of his friends in the group with him. Several of the kids rappelled down the cliff face and into the Zodiac, letting out squeals of victory and delight with their success. Brad had done this several times before, was very confident in his abilities and had long since conquered his fear of the height and challenges that lay before him. I hooked Brad up into the static lines with a 'Figure 8' descending device which he would use to control his descent and allow him to get into a secure rappel position. Before he went over the lip of the cliff, I also connected him to the belay line which was controlled by another instructor, just in case of emergency. Brad made his final climbing calls before going over the edge.

"Belay on. Rappelling!"

With no hesitation or fear, he leaned out backwards over the 70-foot cliff and started his descent with his feet shoulder-width apart and flat on the cliff face. He slowly stepped his way down to the large rock ledge about 15 feet below, then stood straight up before pushing hard off the ledge to drop below the overhang. As the 'cliff master', I was tied in with my rope and harness and was able to lean over the edge of the cliff to observe that all was well and to offer encouragement. As Brad bent his knees to push off and spring out from the rock ledge, I heard a distinct grinding noise and saw a slight shifting of the boulder-sized, horizontal ledge he had just launched from. Brad had already dropped below the ledge, and I lost sight of him. I watched in horror as the refrigerator-sized rock slid from its foundation and plunged down the cliff face, striking Brad on the top of his helmet with a sickening crack. Falling from such a height, the rock finally hit the water with a thunderous, cascading slap and splash! Luke had already steered the zodiac away from the cliff face as a precaution against rocks or debris that could potentially fall during a rappel.

"Brad, are you OK?" I yelled down. He was still out of my sight. I heard him gasping for breath as he responded in a laboured croak,

"Dad, I can't breathe, I think my neck is broken!"

Immediately in rescue mode, I instructed Brad to let go of the ropes so we could lower him with the independent belay rope to the bottom of the cliff. Luke was already maneuvering the Zodiac into place. I quickly gave instructions to the assistant instructor and the rest of the group, then swiftly made my way down the path to the waters' edge. Luke had carefully placed Brad into the Zodiac, unclipped him from all the ropes and then was gently racing to the water's edge to pick me up for the journey to the hospital. A quick radio call to our home base was transferred to 911. We placed Brad on a spine board and I held his head and neck firmly in traction. Luke sped us quickly but very carefully across the water to the closest commercial dock in the town of Chemainus where an ambulance would be waiting. The 40-minute Zodiac trip, seemed like hours as our fears and thoughts swirled with dread for Brad. On arrival at the dock he seemed to be breathing better, but of immense concern were his words, "Dad, I can't feel my feet or toes."

At Chemainus, the waiting ambulance and paramedics firmly strapped Brad onto their spine board so that he could not move and do any further damage. The trip over the water had been rough and risky since we hadn't had any straps to immobilize Brad's neck and spine. After calling my wife, I went with Brad in the ambulance to the hospital and waited as the doctors and nurses wheeled him away for x-rays and examination. My wife, Sandi, arrived and we prayed fervently that God would have mercy on Brad and touch his body in a miraculous way. We experienced deep fear, but also an unmistakable peace, knowing that Brad was in the hands of a God who loved him even more than we did.

It was several hours before the doctor came to speak to us in the waiting room shaking his head in amazement.

"Mr. and Mrs. Riemer, your son is one lucky lad! After x-raying him from many angles, we have concluded that there is actually no permanent spine, neck, or spinal cord damage. We could clearly see compression marks up and down his vertebrae, kind of like an accordion, on the x-rays. He's still young and growing and his bones are still soft, so his spine as well as the stretch of the rope he was attached to, took the force of that heavy rock. Although his spine was compressed, it seems to have rebounded back into its original shape," he said.

"Brad will need to stay in the hospital overnight for observation and will not be able to do any strenuous activity for about three weeks, but after that he should be as good as new!" What a sense of relief and profound thankfulness we felt at that moment! Finally allowed to go to Brad's room, we found him already sitting up in bed with a silly grin on his face.

"Being in the hospital is really cool Mom and Dad, they are letting me eat ice cream and play video games!"

As a family, this experience was, to us, yet another reminder that God is fully aware of all that we do; that He offers His amazing peace, healing and everlasting love to those who trust

Him. This situation could have turned out far worse than it did, and we don't understand why some people experience permanent damage and disability from events like this, while Brad was spared and is living a healthy normal life today. We do know that God sees, hears, and through His divine wisdom, desires to reveal His love and character through any situation, whether miraculous or tragic. In His word, God promises to provide everything we need for life and Godliness. (II Pet 1:3)

I never, ever used that rappel site again! Although I had tried to make it as safe and secure as I possibly could, even my very best was not enough to prevent that terrible accident. I learned many valuable lessons from the experience and to this day I am reminded to seek God's heart and wisdom in everything I do, to rely on Him each day, because He Is Faithful!

Prayer: *Lord Jesus, even though we don't understand why certain things happen, or why some people are spared from serious hardship while others seem to have to endure tremendous difficulties, we are confident that You are faithful, You are loving, and You are able to use any situation to remind us of our need for You! Thank you for being all we need! Amen.*

CUTTHROAT

Camping is unpredictable! Camping is such a wonderful adventure because there is so much in the outdoor environment that we have no control over. When we drive to school, work, or to a soccer practice, we generally just get in the vehicle and go wherever we plan to go, without much expectation of a change to our plans. In the wilderness however, we never know what challenges might be faced on the way to our destination or after we arrive. Heavy rain could wash out the road. A wild animal could stand in our pathway, a wild wind could blow away our tent, or a cold night could chill us to the bone. Even wasps could cause great discomfort by turning an outdoor meal into a swat fest! Hunting and fishing could be exciting and fulfilling, or an exercise in boredom and frustration. I guess that's why over the years I have loved camping, especially in areas that are isolated and mysterious. Since we never know what we'll have to face we must be prepared both mentally and practically for anything.

When he was 11 or 12 years old, I took my oldest son, Luke, on a motorcycle trip to a place where we could camp and fish. On any planned trip like this, we would first sit at the kitchen table and figure out just how much time we had to make the trip. If I had ten days available, we would take a road map and draw a circle indicating a distance requiring 5 days to travel there, and 5 days to get back home. Next, Luke got to decide where he wanted to go within that circle. This time Luke decided he wanted to see Yellowstone National Park in Wyoming, USA. It would only take about three days to get there on the motorcycle, and three days to return home. That would give us four days to explore the canyons, rivers, lakes, wild animals, geysers, thermal 'Paint Pots', and the magnificent, colorful mineral deposits of the Park. We were both excited!

Nearly in Wyoming, we were riding through a canyon highway when the wind unexpectedly gusted so strongly from the side that we were forced to lean into the wind at a sharp angle to prevent getting blown over. It must have looked hilarious to anyone following us since a biker usually only leans over like that when going around a sharp curve.

Another time was on an evening ride. Luke, seated on the back, noticed the sun dropping very low in the sky and shining from the west side, formed a long shadow of us extending across the road. Luke was wearing his motocross helmet with a mouth guard and, with his hands and positioning, was able to create a variety of shapes and characters, kind of like shadow puppets. At one point he tapped me on the back and yelled, "Look Dad!" As I saw the image, I burst out laughing. The shadow of his body and head looked just like 'Daffy Duck' complete with an open bill. Luke even made a loud quacking noise as he moved his hand up and down to simulate Daffy's bill!! What fun we had travelling past spectacular scenery, smelling campfire smoke from campgrounds and fresh-cut wood from sawmills and feeling the wind on our faces.

Finally we arrived at the west gate of Yellowstone National Park! Fees paid, we continued down the highway in search of just the right camping spot to set up the tent where we would spend four exciting days exploring, and fishing the many streams and lakes. Along the roadside we spotted a herd of elk, several buffalo lounging in the sunshine, and a black bear begging for food handouts from tourists who had stopped along the side of the road.

We found a campsite, set up our tent, and prepared a scrumptious supper of Hamburger Helper, soft white buns and iced tea to wash it down. Later, as we sat around the crackling fire, we roasted a pan of 'Jiffy Pop' popcorn which was an annual tradition. As per usual we didn't shake it quite enough and ended up burning the bottom half of the popcorn! After our long day's ride, a good meal and time spent around the campfire, we were bushed and crawled into our sleeping bags. We hung a candle lantern from the ceiling of the tent, which gave us a dim but inviting atmosphere to plan what we might do and see in the days to come. Since we had purchased Park fishing licenses, we also talked about which streams we might try our luck at. After a good chat, a prayer of thanks to God for a great day and safety on the roads, we blew out the candle lantern, and fell into a restful sleep, excited about the days ahead.

Morning welcomed us with bright sunshine and a warm, gentle breeze. Our breakfast of pancakes, syrup, and sausages cooked on our little one-burner stove was soon finished and we loaded up the motorcycle with fishing rods and gear needed for the day. Once on the Park Highway we looked for a lake or stream that might have some fish 'just needing to be caught!' Ten miles down the road, glistening in the sunlight just ahead of us we happened upon a beautiful, clear-blue lake, with a small parking lot. We parked and decided to scout around for a good place to throw in our lines. The shoreline was gravel with a few logs and debris strewn near the edge. There also seemed to be a sharp drop off which meant that we would be able to get our lures quite deep to hopefully attract some rainbow or lake trout.

There was only one vehicle in the parking lot when we arrived, and we spoke to the man who was just getting into his truck to leave. When we asked him how the fishing was, he frowned and said he had been fishing for a couple of hours and had not gotten even a nibble. He was pulling out to try somewhere else. Undeterred, Luke and I chose our own spots on the shore of the lake and cast our lines into the deep water. After half an hour of casting and getting no bites or nibbles, Luke decided to scout around the lake some more to see it he could find a more promising place to throw in his line. I watched him as he walked about a quarter of the way around the small lake and stopped at a log that rested on the shore but stuck far out into the lake. As I watched, Luke stepped up on the log, which seemed firmly embedded on the shore, and carefully walked further out onto it. The log bobbed gently in the water under his seventy-five pounds. Luke had a good sense of balance, so although the log moved, jiggled, and bobbed, he was able to make his way securely out onto the deep water without falling in. Once out on the log, Luke looked down into the water and yelled loudly that he could see a large school of good-sized fish gathered below the submerged end of the log. I yelled back that he should drop and jig his line to see if any of them would take the lure. Luke braced himself on the narrow end of that log and dropped his line down into the school of fish. Within only a few seconds, a fish took the lure! Luke let out a hoot and holler, and, since his footing was somewhat tenuous, instead of reeling in his catch, he simply walked back on the log to shore with the fish still on his line. Once on solid ground he reeled in the fish which was a sight to see! He had landed a beautiful, two- pound cut throat trout, with gorgeous blue-green coloring on its body and a distinctive red colored slash just below its head. What a fish! And there were more where that one came from! Luke got a long green willow stick and laced the fish onto the stick through its mouth and gills, and then stuck the stick in the shallow water to keep the fish fresh, while he went back out onto the log to try for another. Within a couple of minutes, he hooted again and walked down the log back to shore with his second fish, once again lacing it onto his willow 'Fish Stick'. Meanwhile, I stood on the shore casting my line out into deep water without getting so much as a nibble. Luke had found the perfect spot, the perfect technique and was perfectly light and nimble enough to walk out on that log to where the fish were plentiful.

Luke now had three large fish stuck on his willow stick. A car entered the parking area and a man walked over to where Luke was fishing.

"Any luck son?" he asked.

Luke proudly showed the man his fish and told him that they were biting just fine! The man's eyes lit up. He quickly returned to the vehicle and told his two buddies about this amazing fishing spot. Within minutes the three were casting into the lake and before long other vehicles began to fill the parking lot. Luke just kept hauling in until his limit was reached - six large cutthroat trout, strung up and ready for cleaning. Other larger, heavier fishermen, attempted to balance on Luke's log but the uneasy log would sink below the lake surface and they would return to shore empty-handed. The entire time we remained there we did not see even one other person catch a fish, or even acknowledge a nibble. Luke, happy and thankful for his good fortune, proudly carried his 6-fish willow stick around like an Olympic gold medal!

As we were packing up the motorcycle in readiness for the ride back to camp, a plump, older man approached Luke and his mess of fish and asked if Luke would mind if he held the stick to have his wife take a video of him.

"Sure." Luke said as he laughed.

The man took the stick which was heavily loaded with those six beautiful fish. His wife pointed the video camera toward him.

"OK, Hon, we're rolling," she said. The man spoke loudly and with a southern accent. His words came out something like this:

"Well, Earl, d'ya remember before me and Blanch left home, we told you we were going to Yellowstone National Park to do some fishing and catch us some big ones? You said we were crazy and would never catch anything except maybe an old boot or a tire. Earl, feast yer eyes on this mess of fish I just caught. Never doubt me again, old buddy! See ya when we get home."

Finished with the video, they asked what we were going to do with our catch. I really hadn't given much thought to the future of the fish, but we had no place to keep them, and there was no way we could eat 12 or 13 pounds of fish at once. The woman asked if we had everything needed to prepare a good meal of fish and I responded that all we had was a frying pan.

"Oh," she said, "you need to wrap them in tin foil with lots of butter, salt and pepper, potatoes, onions and some vegetables and nestle them in the hot coals of your fire for about 15-20 minutes. Then you'll have an amazing meal." Since we didn't have any of those items, the woman offered to go into their RV, and get everything we would need - if only we would share the fish with them! Great idea! Luke and I kept two of the catch for our own good eating, and gave the others to the couple 'cause they had a fridge and could keep the fish fresh. What a feast we had that night, and what a story to tell when we got home!

Catching those fish, kind of reminds me of faith in Jesus! Many folk want the life that Jesus offers. They see Jesus followers who know they are loved and forgiven, that have thankful hearts, purpose, and a sense of belonging, and then those folk try to claim or earn those things without realizing that they are available through Jesus alone! Some will even try to mimic what they see a Jesus-follower do, without knowing the Bible says, "Unless you become like little children, you will never enter the kingdom of heaven." Matthew 18:3. They are just like the man who took credit for catching Luke's fish, but it was just a lie. Jesus is available to anyone who will humble himself, and simply come to Him in faith.

Prayer: *Lord Jesus, thanks for making a way for us to receive the treasure of Your life, (kind of like that log out to the fish) and for reminding us that You are 'the Way, the Truth and the Life' and that no one can come to the Father except through You! John 14:6 Amen.*

Electric
WONDER
PEN
Wood
Burning

CHRISTMAS LESSONS
PART 1: FROM THE WISHBOOK

Don't you love Christmas? I sure do. I love all the decorations, and the Christmas carols and music everywhere. I love having family and friends who visit and share meals, and the church programs that remind us that the whole celebration is about Jesus... the greatest Gift ever given! When I was a kid, my parents taught me about Jesus and how God sent His only Son to earth as a great gift of love for me, but I was often more interested in what I would get out of it. I loved to wake up early on Christmas morning to see all the gifts under the tree and wonder how long I would have to wait until everyone else got up to open the presents. I always kept track of the gifts under the tree long before Christmas morning came around. As soon as the tree went up and the first gifts got wrapped and placed under it, I made it my business to know who each present was for, how heavy it was and who it was from. If it was from my Grandma and Grandpa, it was probably a pair of socks or a sweater. If it was from one of my brothers or my sister it likely wasn't a very expensive gift, because they didn't have much money.

By the middle of October each fall, the Sears Catalogue would arrive in the mailbox. This catalogue, called 'The Wish Book', was full of pictures of toys, games, bikes, footballs, baseball gloves, skateboards and all kinds of things to hope for. When you wanted something from that catalogue, you just had to get your mom or dad to call the phone number in the book, place the order, and then it would arrive at the store in a week or two. Then you would have to go to the store, pay for the item and take it home. I loved the Wish Book and would flip through it almost every day, imagining what it would be like to get some of that cool stuff.

You needed to tell your mom and dad what you wanted for Christmas way ahead of time though, because they would have to order it from the catalogue so that it would arrive in time to be wrapped and put under the tree. I usually told my parents what I wanted by the middle of November so that they would have lots of time to get it. It was fun to see newly wrapped gifts take their place under the tree and try to guess if it was one of the things I had asked for. One year I saw a 'Deluxe Wood

Burning Set' in the Wish Book and it looked so cool! It had a hot wood burning tool, kind of like an electric pencil with a thick cork band around it so that you wouldn't burn your hand when you were using it. It also had four or five different tips that you could put on it for burning different designs on the wood. The set included a selection of plywood pieces of different sizes with outlines of pictures on them, such as a horse with a cowboy riding it, or a pot of flowers, or a racing car speeding down a track. If you plugged in the burning tool and got it hot enough, you could trace and burn the outline of the picture. I wanted that wood burning set 'Baaaaaaad' and showed my mom the picture in the catalogue. I knew it cost quite a bit, but if I didn't ask for a lot of other stuff, maybe they would get it for me.

I waited and hoped and hoped and waited. Finally, around the first week of December on a Saturday, when I knew that my folks were doing some late shopping, they came home after I had already gone to bed. I wondered if they had ordered and picked up that wood burning set for me.

The next day, I waited until my mom was busy in the

kitchen and my dad was out in the garage, and since there were no new gifts placed under the tree, I snuck into their bedroom. Mom and Dad had a closet with a sliding door which made a rolling rumbling sound when it was opened. I closed their bedroom door behind me and then ever so carefully, I slowly slid their closet door open. My heart was beating so fast I could hear it in my head... maybe because of the excitement of discovering the wood burning set, or maybe because I was afraid that they would hear the closet door opening and catch me in the act! Once the door was opened, I looked up on the high shelf, where they sometimes hid stuff we weren't supposed to see, but it didn't seem to be there. Next, I checked the ends of the closet where my mom stacked extra boxes of summer clothes, and my dad kept his hunting gear and shotgun... no wood burning set. Finally, I checked up against the wall behind all their clothes that were hanging up. I found a box that was already wrapped up and it looked to be about the right size and shape for a wood burning set, so ever so carefully, I took it out and laid it on their bed. My heart was now almost beating out of my chest. I was so scared that they would hear something and open the door, but my curiosity was too strong! I had to know what was in that box! I pulled the tape back on one end of the parcel. It ripped a little bit, but I figured I could fix it when I put the tape back on. Thankfully, my parents didn't like to use much tape, so there were only three small pieces to pull off. When I pulled the wrapping paper on the end of the box back, I could see the end of the box with the label: "Deluxe Wood Burning Set!" 'Yesssssss' I thought, and quickly, but very carefully, I folded the paper back the way it was and stuck the tape back in place before returning the box to its hiding place behind Mom and Dad's clothes.

A funny thing happened over the next three weeks before Christmas morning came. I knew what I was getting, but because I had spoiled the surprise, I wasn't really looking forward to getting the wood burning set any more like I was before. In fact, when I looked through the Wish Book, I found things that I wanted even more than the Wood Burning Set. I felt guilty every time I saw that box under the tree because I knew what I had done by sneaking into my parents' room. When Christmas morning came, I hated having to open that present, pretending that I was surprised and happy to get it. I remember burning two or three of the pictures and then I lost interest and it ended up going to the Salvation Army Thrift Store a few months later. I had ruined the surprise. I felt guilty for my actions, and I was not even thankful that my parents had paid the money to get me what I asked for. I felt guilty and ashamed. One thing was for sure . . . I would never do that again!

It's pretty normal for us to make mistakes and do things that we wish we hadn't done, but those mistakes can turn into lessons if we lay them at Jesus feet, and let Him transform us. On that Christmas so long ago, I learned that surprise was part of the gift that was taken away by my own thoughtless manipulation. I tried to make things happen just as I wanted, instead of allowing things to happen the way they were meant to happen.

When we try to get our own way, and don't consider anyone else, we end up hurting other people and ultimately, ourselves, and we rob ourselves of the joy of living life with anticipation one day at a time. Jesus tells us:

"Don't be anxious for your life, saying 'What shall we eat?' or

'What shall we drink?' or 'What shall we wear?', for your heavenly Father knows that you need them. But seek first his kingdom and his righteousness, and all these things will be given to you as well. Therefore, do not worry about tomorrow, for tomorrow will worry about itself."

Matt 6:31-34

Prayer: *Jesus, I'm sorry that sometimes I run ahead and try to get my own way, without considering that You have my very best interest in mind. Help me to look forward to what You have in store for me and to learn to value the surprises that come my way, as I trust in You. Amen.*

CHRISTMAS LESSONS
PART 2: THE MOCCASINS

Once again a valuable Christmas Lesson was learned. I was 10 years old. At that time we lived in Edmonton, Alberta, which is extremely cold in the winter. We always had lots of snow and loved to go tobogganing, skating, and building snowmen and snow forts in our back yard.

Lots of kids wore moccasins or 'Mukluks' to school, kind of like the ones I had seen in pictures of Eskimos in library books. The boots were made of smooth, waterproof leather with no soles, and some had neat tassels around the top that flipped and twirled when you ran. The moccasins went about half way up to your knees and had long laces to tie them tight on your legs. With moccasins you could play in deep snow without any of that cold wet stuff getting into your boots.

Yup, I needed a pair of Mukluks for Christmas. I found just the right picture in the Sears Christmas Wish Book and told Mom and Dad that those moccasins were really the only thing I wanted for Christmas. Have you ever noticed that when you want something really badly, you start to see them everywhere? Kids were wearing them to school. People in the grocery store, on the sledding hill, at church, even people on TV were wearing the exact moccasins that I wanted. My desire for a pair of Mukluks was becoming unhealthy, and it finally exploded on Christmas Day!

For several weeks I was thinking about moccasins, asking for moccasins, seeing people of all ages wearing moccasins, and wishing I had a pair of moccasins, and then Christmas Day arrived. I couldn't help but see there was only one present with my name on it under the tree, so it had to be what I wanted so badly. When all the gifts were passed out, and it was my turn to open my present, I wildly tore off the wrapping paper from the box that looked like it could actually contain my dream pair of Mukluks. Boy oh boy oh boy ooh boy!!! With great excitement, I opened the box and peered inside, then pulled out a pair of . . . leather boots.

They kind of looked like Moccasins, but they were not the ones I had been dreaming about. These were not the smooth light-colored leather I wanted, but darker and fuzzier. They didn't have long laces all the way up, but instead had some colored bead work on them and a top collar of leather with tassels all the way around. The color and texture were just so different than what I had imagined. My heart sank, and I'm sure my eyes showed my disappointment. Then I spoke words to my Mom and Dad that were disrespectful, demeaning and accusing.

"Well, I guess you guys couldn't afford to get me a new pair, eh?" I said. My Dad, the hurt showing on his face, moved over to where I was sitting and took the box from my hands.

"Del, Mom and I knew just how much you wanted a particular pair of moccasins. We looked all over town to find just the right ones, and then came across this pair which actually cost twice as much as the other kind that you saw in the Sears Catalogue. These are actually made by the Eskimo people up north who hand stitched them, designed the beads on them, and made them extra thick so that they would keep your feet warm and dry. The leather is a special kind that is not as light and smooth as the ones you have seen, but is of a higher quality and is what they actually use up North." Then Dad continued in a sad but stern tone of voice.

"I'm sorry, Del, that you don't like these Mukluks that we spent so much time and money on, and that you don't appreciate what we did for you. Because of your disrespect and ungrateful attitude, we are going to return these moccasins and get our money back. Unfortunately, you need to learn a lesson in being thankful for what you get, and you will not be getting any other present this Christmas. Now go to your room, think about your attitude, and ask God to forgive you and change your heart."

I gave the box back to my Dad and shuffled to my room in tears, tears of regret for saying what I had to my parents, tears of sadness because I would not get anything for Christmas, and tears that made me wish I could go back and open that gift all over again. I wanted to ask my parents to explain the story behind the moccasins that they had so lovingly bought for me. Once I understood they were actually much better than what I had asked for, I wanted these leather ones even more than the ones everyone else had... but it was too late. All I got that Christmas was a valuable lesson that has served me well through my life.

We don't always get exactly what we want, but sometimes what God gives us is much better than what we even asked for. In the Bible we are told. "In everything give thanks," I Thess 5:8, and that "Every good and perfect gift is from above, coming down from the Father of lights." (God Himself!) James 1:17.

Even though it was a very difficult lesson to learn, it became one of the best Christmas gifts I have ever received. Many years later I told that story to my wife (Grandma). She felt so bad for me that she went out and bought a pair of moccasins that still hang on the wall in our rec. room, a reminder of the lesson God taught me, way back when I was just 10.

Prayer: *Dear Jesus, thanks for loving me. Thanks for using the people in my life who love me to teach me lessons I need to learn. And God, help me to not want what someone else has instead of being thankful for what I have. Amen.*

HE DROPPED IT RIGHT IN MY LAP

I am a Pastor! Even pastors get discouraged sometimes. Have you ever been discouraged and felt like things were hopeless and everyone was against you? A few years ago, while experiencing a particularly difficult time, that's exactly the way I felt. I was feeling criticized and under stress because of taking on too many things at once. It was time to recharge my emotional and physical 'batteries'! As a hunter, fisherman, and outdoorsman, the wilderness is the best place for me to go when a break is needed because it is usually quiet with few distractions or interruptions. I love the restful sound of the wind in the trees and the birds' light-hearted chirping and singing, as if they didn't have a worry in the world.

I love to watch how God's creation obeys and does exactly what the Creator tells it to do. In the fall season, leaves dramatically change in the dying process from green to yellow to brown, drift to the ground, decompose, and then create rich soil for the next season of growth. Spring arrives; tiny buds slowly emerge from tree branches exhibiting vibrant color and life through the forest. This is all by God's design. I marvel how creation obeys its Creator but man often tries to carve out his own way, rejecting God's directions by trying to control things himself. We are told to love one another, to give preference to one another, to sacrifice for one another, to be patient with one another, and yet these are so hard to do when our natural tendency is to just look out for ourselves.

In the wilderness that fall day, I felt like people had let me down and I needed some time to refocus. I even told God what I wanted from Him that day.

"God, I've been going through a hard time lately and I need You to refresh me in the beauty of your outdoor creation, and here's how I would like this to happen. I'm going to the top of Monroe Mountain to the lake where I've been before. You know I've caught lots of fish and enjoyed times of peace and refreshment there so this is what I would like You to do for me. Could You please make sure it is sunny and warm because I need that warm, comforting embrace from You. Next, God, could You make sure I catch lots of fish, because it will remind me that You are for me and that You are in control. You have said in your Word that You ". . . will provide all my needs according to (Your) riches in Glory," Phil 4:19 so that's what I'm counting on God! Thank you. Amen." (If you're thinking, that instead of resting in the love of Jesus who knew what I needed that day, that I was taking control and simply telling God what He should do, well, you are right!)

I got up very early that next morning and headed to Mount Monroe. It was a pretty cloudy beginning but I figured once I started up the mountain I would drive above the clouds and then be bathed in warm sunshine. Wrong! The higher my truck climbed the thicker and more dense the clouds became. By the time I reached the lake, everything was completely fogged in along with a light drizzle of rain and a temperature that was quickly dropping to downright cold. Not quite what I had asked for, but my thoughts persisted that perhaps things would change. Since I had come all this way, and needed to trust in God, I might as well get into my inflatable boat and do some fishing.

My fishing boat, the 'Fish Cat', is a small inflatable vessel with two pontoons that can be blown up by mouth. The pontoons are in a 'U' shape, circling around the seat with an opening in the front. I climbed into a pair of 'hip waders' and fastened swim fins onto my feet. The seat of the 'Fish Cat' is above water level but my lower legs and fins are below the water so, once seated, my fins enable me to navigate around the lake. This little vessel keeps me very close to the water and makes fly fishing and spin casting very easy and enjoyable. Even though it was cold and raining, I had my rain jacket on and my wide brim hat would keep the water out of my face. With my lower legs in the water propelling my boat, I was warm and still optimistic that there may yet be some fish to be caught.

While propelling the boat slowly around the lake with my fins, I am able to cast my 'spin-caster' line and let it 'troll' deep down in the water, and then affix the rod into its holder. Then I am able to take my 'Fly Rod' and cast in an arc around my boat to attract fish closer to the surface. Many pleasurable hours and days have produced lots of fish using this technique. Much to my annoyance, this was not one of those pleasurable days!

After three or four hours of propelling myself around the lake in drenching rain, and without so much as a nibble on either of my lines, I became more discouraged and annoyed and increasingly angry with God. Here I was, a pastor, trying my best to do what God had asked me to do even in difficult circumstances. All I needed was for God to give me a nice warm day, under a blue sky with lots of fish taking my hooks, to restore my confidence and confirm to me that God was aware of me, that He valued my efforts and held me in His embrace. But instead, I was cold, wet, and miserable and had just wasted all this time trusting that God would give me what I needed!

Frustrated and depressed, all I could say in honesty was, "Thanks a lot God. Thanks for nothing." I decided to just give up and pack it in for the day. I slowly kicked my way back to shallow water and reeled in my fly line, placing that rod in the holder on my boat. Then I began to reel in my spin caster line which had been trolling in deep water but now was making its way through the shallow water to my rod before I brought my inflatable boat to the shoreline for removal. In frustration with my situation and God's apparent uncaring attitude about me,

I reeled in my line quickly. As the lure came out of the water and I reached over to place the rod into its holder, a miraculous thing happened. A 17-inch trout that had apparently been following the fast-moving hook, leaped high out of the water in an effort to grab the lure and landed perfectly in my lap without ever actually touching the lure! I was shocked and surprised at what lay squirming and flipping in my lap. I grabbed the fish and knocked it on the head with the 'bonker' I keep in my gear pocket, then stared in disbelief at the fish in my lap and considered what had just happened.

I realized that although I had told God what I wanted Him to do, He did what He knew I needed Him to do. I began to understand that life is full of challenges and hard times, and that God has things to teach us in the middle of those difficulties. If He just made our situation easier and more comfortable, we would likely not learn the things we needed to. God showed me clearly that day that sometimes we go through miserable and hard times, but He is certainly aware of our circumstances and loves us through those times. He taught me not to always ask for what I want, but for what He wants, and that I should watch and listen for His answer. Even Jesus when going to the cross said, "Not my will but Yours be done." Luke 22: 42. It's also pretty cool, that God uses His creation, like weather, lakes, and fish, to teach us lessons that we need to learn!

Prayer: *Lord Jesus, I'm sorry for expecting You to do everything my way. Thank You for teaching me in ways that get my attention and draw my heart to trust You in every situation. Oh, and God... help me to learn to obey You even like that fish did! Amen.*

CHAPTER 16

THE PARKING SPOT

Of course you've never done anything wrong that you thought would make other people think you were doing something right. Right?

I guess it's kind of like 'lying' to make people think you are telling the truth when you're really not. I know we figure that is what kids do, and that adults are beyond that kind of nonsense. Sadly, all of us want people to think well of us no matter what our age, and we can readily talk ourselves into lying or deception when it makes us feel better about ourselves or how we think others view us. Once, as a high school student, I told my parents that I was going with my school friend, Dave, to the Open House of a local Technical School to see all the science experiments and projects on display. My parents, pleased that I was going to an educational event, gladly gave me permission to go. Dave and I actually planned to sneak into a 'restricted' movie with no intention of going to the school. We didn't want to lie about what we were doing so we drove to the Technical School, walked in the door only to walk right back out again; that way, we could assure our parents that we had actually gone, as promised, and we wouldn't be lying! We did just as planned, walked in and out of the school, drove to the theatre, and watched a movie that our parents would never have given permission to see. When I got home, my parents asked how the Open House had been, and I told them that it had been very interesting! (Did I lie, or not?) You would think that this kind of deception would not be a temptation once I grew older and more mature. If you think that, then you would be wrong!

It was just a few years ago that I was taking my disabled wife, Sandi, to Winners, a clothing store in a nearby city. We pulled into the handicap parking space right near the front door of the store. Because Sandi finds walking difficult, we have a parking permit to hang on the rear-view mirror in the car. That permit allows us to park in places specially marked for people with a mobility handicap. Using the wheelchair stored in the car trunk, I wheeled Sandi into the store where we shopped for some clothes. It is difficult and tiring for Sandi to try on clothing in the store change-rooms so we often buy a few items which are later tried on at home, and then we return the ones that don't fit or are not suitable for her. This is what we did that day. We bought several items for her to try on at home. She decided to keep two of the items and I would return the remaining ones.

A couple of days later I drove our car back to Winners to return the items Sandi did not want. It was a busy day at the shopping center and the parking lot was full of cars. As I drove around and around looking for a parking spot, impatient and in a bit of a hurry, I stopped and looked at the empty handicap space that was right near the front door of the store. I was actually not allowed to park in that spot if my wife was not in the car with me. As I sat in my car contemplating that empty parking space, my mind started to justify what I was about to do. Here is what I was thinking: "Since, the items I was returning were for a handicapped person, it should be okay to park here. Besides, I wouldn't be very long in the store."

I convinced myself that even though I was wrong, I could justify my action and appease my guilty conscience. (Kind of like what I did back in High School by walking into the 'Open

House' and then walking right back out again, just to say I had been there!) The problem was, as an adult, and especially as a Pastor of a church, I needed to set a good example of integrity and truthfulness.

I parked, and made sure the permit was hanging clearly visible on the mirror before getting out of the car. My conscience was talking to me and I could hear a voice inside my head saying "Del, you are not handicapped. If people see you walking nimbly into the store they will know you cheated and took that spot just because you don't want to walk across the entire parking lot to get to the store. Others might see your handicap permit, observe you walking normally, and think you stole it just to get close to the store."

Although I am embarrassed to tell you this, the next thing I did was hobble toward the doors of the store, dragging one foot behind me as though I had a serious disability and was indeed handicapped. Once I got into the front doors, I checked to see that no one was looking, and reverted to walking normally and quickly up to the counter to return my wife's clothing items. All this time, I was feeling guilty and ashamed for trying to deceive people and I understood that the only one I was deceiving was myself! I realized that God not only saw me pathetically limping into the store, He saw my lie as I tried to make myself look good while compromising my integrity. I had a vision of God in my mind, looking down at me while shaking His head with sadness and disappointment. This vision was a result of my own guilt and regret not God's actual response to my actions. He knows we're not perfect and make foolish mistakes but He only looks at us with love, favour, and forgiveness. This love give us the freedom to be honest before Him and not live in fear or guilt. God isn't waiting to punish us for our sin, Jesus came and paid that price long ago. Even though this event still causes me embarrassment and regret, it has become a great lesson which serves me well to this day.

Often, we want others to see us the way we want to be seen, even if it is not who we really are. People are usually okay with the truthful revelation of our personal weaknesses because they experience weaknesses and insecurities too. It gives them permission to be honest as well. Ultimately, God knows our hearts and our natural tendencies and loves us anyway. He wants to change us into the kind of people who reflect His image through all of life's choices, words and actions.

Perhaps you have some things you need to confess and ask forgiveness for. Once you do that, it opens up a wonderful freedom to be the person God desires you to be.

Prayer: *Lord, I know that I can't fool You or hide anything from You. Thank you for loving me the way that I am, and for working in my heart so that I can be increasingly honest and authentic in all I do and say. Amen.*

GUS FOR LUNCH

Years ago, employed by a Christian organization that worked with youth who were in trouble with the law, I had to travel to other cities and colleges in search of candidates who could come on staff with us. One time this responsibility took me to Saskatoon, Saskatchewan. There was a Bible School just north of the city and I had to speak at an assembly there about our ministry. While in Saskatoon, I stayed at a hotel and in some of my free time, I wandered around the beautiful river valley and went back to familiar sights from a time, years before, when I used to live in Saskatoon. I had always loved the walking trails and benches that are located behind the old and elegant Bessborough Hotel because they meander through parkland areas and reveal a spectacular view of the river valley below.

On this morning, as I walked those trails, I found a well-placed park bench to sit on where I could think, pray, and admire the view. I thought about how our organization engaged with kids who struggled with school, and whose parents didn't know how to deal with their behavior and rebellion. Some of the youth we worked with had run away from home. Some were involved in crime. Others had skipped out of school. They were sent to us to learn how to behave and become responsible young people. I thought about people who do not have a loving mother and father, or who have gone through very difficult times which have left them angry, hopeless and alone. As I sat on that park bench thinking of all the problems that so many people deal with, I remember praying that God would use me to offer people kindness, acceptance and love. Although I didn't realize it at the time, God was about to teach me a valuable lesson in what it can cost to love and care for others. Jesus was kind, caring and loving, and even healed the sick, but many people didn't understand Him. They abused Him, and the ultimate price He paid was death on a cross.

As I sat and prayed, I asked God to love people through me. When I looked up, I saw an elderly man staggering down the pathway towards me, dressed in old worn out clothes that were filthy dirty. He smelled very bad, even from a distance. His face was unshaven and there seemed to be food or dirt caked into his beard. He wore an old hat with a brim around it, and the hair that tumbled out from under it was stringy and greasy looking. He was pulling a squeaky, two-wheeled cart behind him that was full of his worldly belongings. He mumbled as he walked, and I could see his brown teeth and drool dripping in long strings from his lips. The smell of his dirty clothes was a sour mix of stale urine and alcohol and it got stronger as he got closer to my bench. As the man staggered up to my bench with his eyes glassy and half closed, he paused right in front of me.

"Hey buddy, can you give me five bucks?" he slurred. My natural inclination was to respond with, "Sorry Mister, I don't have any money for you," hoping he would just shuffle away. But a very clear and authoritative voice echoed through my mind at that very moment. I knew immediately that God was getting my attention and saying to me, "Del, you just finished asking me to love people through you, and this is the person I want you to love." Almost before I realized it, I said: "Sir, I am not going to just give you money, but if you are hungry, I'd like to buy you a meal, would that be okay?"

"Okay, let's go eat!" he replied, after pausing for a moment to think as he swayed on his feet. I stood up and walked slowly along the path beside him as he pulled his cart and we made our way toward one of the main downtown streets where several restaurants were located. The smell of the man was almost overpowering, and I tried to breathe through my mouth to avoid gagging. We came to a fast-food restaurant where I thought we might find a place to sit well away from the other customers.

I opened the door for the man, and he pulled his cart through the door as well. He sat down at a table right in the middle of the restaurant, standing his cart up next to the table. I noticed that every eye in the place was staring at us, and a few people even got up and moved to tables further away from us. I asked the man his name.

"Gus," he replied. I asked him what he'd like for lunch, but he didn't seem to know what he wanted, he didn't look up at the menu on the wall behind the ordering counter either, so I wondered if he couldn't see very well, or perhaps he couldn't read.

"Well, Gus," I said, "would you just like me to order for you? Would you like a full hamburger meal with fries and a drink?"

"Sure," Gus replied. I asked what kind of drink he liked.

"Cola," he said.

"Sure thing. Comin' right up." I went up to the counter and ordered deluxe hamburgers with fries and Cokes for both of us. After paying for the meals, I returned to the table, although the strong odor coming from Gus almost made me linger a little longer at the cashier's counter. As we sat and waited for our meal, I asked Gus where he was from and if he had any family in the area. "Born on the reservation outside of town," seemed to be all he could say. I asked several other questions and tried to get him to share a bit about his life, but his face was turned down to the floor as he slumped in his chair, fidgeted with his fingers and remained silent. I tried my best to make small talk with Gus, and told him what I was doing in Saskatoon, and that I used to live in the city many years before when I was a travelling musician. Gus just looked at the floor and didn't say a word.

Finally, our order number was called, and I went up to the counter to claim the trays of food. I put one tray in front of Gus and sat down at the table across from him. The very moment I placed his food on the table, he grabbed the hamburger and began to stuff it into his mouth as if he had not eaten for weeks. It almost looked as though he was just taking huge bites and then swallowing them whole! Mustard and ketchup were leaking out of his mouth and running down his beard but he didn't seem to notice or care. I think he finished his burger in about four bites, and then devoured his fries four or five at a time. When he drank his Coke, he drank so fast that the pop ran out of the corners of his mouth, down his beard and onto his coat and pants. Gus didn't say a word but finished all his food in just over a minute. The other customers in the restaurant were staring and I could hear some gasping and whispering. I had barely started my meal, when Gus finished his.

"Is there more?" he asked.

"Sure Gus, do you want a full meal again or just another burger?"

"Burger and drink," he said, and then looked down at the floor again without taking any time to wipe the mustard, ketchup and pop off his face and coat. I went back to the counter and ordered another deluxe hamburger and drink and returned to start eating my meal. When his second meal arrived, Gus once again crammed the burger into his mouth and gulped down the drink in less than a minute, and even the restaurant staff were now watching. I didn't know how to respond to all the disgusted looks and shaking heads of the people who must have wondered who I was and why I would bring this man into the restaurant. In my embarrassment and self-consciousness, I tried not to make eye contact with anyone.

Once Gus finished his second meal, I asked if he wanted anything else, and all he said was, "ice cream!" The restaurant sold soft ice cream cones, so I went to the counter and purchased one. When I gave it to Gus, he crammed it into his mouth, getting some in his mouth and the rest dribbled into his beard and began running down his chin onto his shirt, jacket and chest. What a sight Gus had become. I thought he was dirty and unkempt when I first met him, but it was much worse now! I asked if there was anything else, he wanted.

"Yes! Now I want my five bucks!" He spoke loudly in a slurred, angry tone. I told Gus that, as I had said before, I would not just give him money, but if he was still hungry, I would be happy to get him more food. He stood up from the table, and using his arm swept both our trays off the table and onto the floor with a loud crash as food and debris spread all around our table. He then yelled at me loudly and angrily, calling me many nasty and vulgar names. As he spewed cuss words and fury at me, tiny pieces of food and spit flew from his mouth and he staggered backwards toward the door. With one final barrage of slurred swear words, Gus, dragging his cart behind him disappeared out the door, and I never saw him again. In the quiet, I was stunned, as was everyone else in the restaurant. I didn't say a word, tried not to make eye contact with anyone, but just picked up the mess left on the floor, placed it into the garbage container by the door and slipped out of the restaurant

I made my way to a quiet place in a nearby park, sat on a bench, dropped my head in my hands and sobbed uncontrollably.

"God, what was the point of that? You asked me to love that man and treat him with kindness and respect, so I did, and this is what I get? Not only did he not appreciate what I did for him, he hated and abused me!" The next words that God spoke into my heart have stuck with me ever since and I will never forget the lesson God taught me that day. Here is what I heard in my heart.

"Del, what you just went through was not intended for Gus, but for YOU! You now have a small idea of what I (Jesus) went through for you. When I walked this earth, I was misunderstood, accused and abused, and I even gave up My life because I love mankind. There will be times when you will do the best you can, and you'll treat people with love and tell them the truth, but they will not accept it. They may even accuse and mistreat you. Just remember that in the long run, love wins. Keep your eyes on me, trust me, listen to my voice, and let me use you to love those around you. And remember, I love you Del!"

So, when you do the right thing and love people because you

love God, don't worry if people don't respond the way you want them to. When we love and obey Jesus, He reminds us that our life is all about our relationship with Him. "Love one another as I have loved you!" John 15:12

Prayer: *Dear Jesus, thank You for loving me even when I don't respond the way I should. Help me to see people the way You see them, instead of judging people from what they look like on the outside. Remind me Lord that You love everyone the same no matter what, and You want me to love them that way too! Amen.*

143

BEAR IN THE YARD

Living in the little town of Hedley for a time, we experienced life very differently from living in the city. Our house was located at the top of 'Hospital Hill', right on the outskirts of town. We had 12 fruit trees in our yard, and frequent, wandering visitors such as deer, bear, raccoons and squirrels. Because we lived so high up, Brad and Luke would get on their bikes each morning and coast down the road, gathering incredible speed, making it all the way to the little school house without even pedalling! We lived not far from 20 Mile Creek, where our two boys would swim or fish, and in the mid-winter freeze we would skate on the creek. Christmas time was the occasion for driving down the snow-covered road that followed 20 Mile Creek, to look for that special tree to cut down and bring home.

On one of those Christmas-time trips, we found an old Volkswagen car hood with bullet holes in it laying in the ditch alongside the road. We turned the hood upside down to create a make-shift toboggan, laid a folded blanket in it to cover up the sharp metal edges made by the bullet holes, and towed the boys down the road as fast as we dared to go. When just the right Christmas tree had been found and cut down, we laid it on that old car hood, and towed it home. Hedley was the perfect place for our sons to grow up and learn to love the outdoors and all the adventures and lessons it had to teach them.

There was a neighbor lady who lived not far from our house with her small pet dog. One day, the lady took her little dog out into the back yard to pee and came face to face with a male black bear feeding on fallen fruit from trees in her yard. Startled, the bear reared up on its hind legs to defend itself and then charged toward the lady and her dog. Holding the dog in her arms, the terrified lady ran as fast as she could back to the house with the bear following right behind her. She slammed the door behind her just as the bear arrived and clawed at the wood panel and window. Really scared, and knowing that I was a hunter, the lady phoned, told me about the aggressive bear in her yard and begged me to shoot it. When I arrived at the house, the bear had already left and was nowhere in sight.

Because it's not legal to shoot a firearm within town limits, I first had to get special permission from the BC Conservation Office to shoot the bear. I called and told them of the aggressive bear within our town limit that had actually charged a lady and her dog. The Officer on the phone was very understanding and asked me many questions; he wanted to know our exact location in town and if I was an experienced hunter. When I told the officer that I hunted moose, deer and bear every year, he said that since hunting season was only four days away, he would give me a special permit to shoot the bear within town limits once the season opened. I now had four days to prepare how I would hunt the wild black bear right in my own back yard!

Because of the aggressive nature of this nuisance bear, I was permitted to 'bait' it. Baiting meant I could draw him to a food source in our own yard so I would have a clear shot at him without putting any houses or populated areas in the line of the shot. Since there were several fruit trees on our property, and a bright yard light to illuminate the area, I placed some fruit in a bucket where it could be easily seen and smelled by the bear at night. (A bear's sense of smell is 2100 times stronger than a human's.) We had a second-story sundeck on the end of our house which would give me a perfect vantage point to see the fruit bucket and the bear illuminated by the yard light. With hunting season still a few days away, I placed that bucket of fruit in the same location nightly to get the bear used to finding an easy food source. Sure enough, it was empty every morning. Now for the final climax of our clever plan!

It was Opening Day of bear hunting season, and the first day we could legally shoot the bear that had charged our neighbour. Since we lived in a small town of only 400 people, word had quickly gotten around town about what I was going to do to eliminate the aggressive bear. Many townsfolk with small children or pets, who were also afraid of being attacked, wished me good luck with my plan.

One of the problems with the plan of drawing the bear to the fruit bucket was that we had no idea when the animal would actually show up! My son, Luke, and I devised a clever plan, which in hindsight, perhaps was not as clever as we thought it was. Luke was about 10 years old and excited to be part of this big adventure. We decided to put our sleeping bags out on the deck of the house and sleep out there until the bear arrived for his fruit snack. To alert us as to when he arrived, we tied a string to the handle of the fruit bucket and ran it up onto the deck where Luke and I would be sleeping. We tied the other end of the string to Luke's big toe. When the bear nosed into the bucket and knocked it over, the string should tug on Luke's toe and wake him up. Luke would then wake me up; I would pick up my loaded rifle by my sleeping bag, simply find the bear in my rifle scope and BOOM, dead Bear! (Okay, okay. I know what you're thinking: "What if the bear takes the bucket away and drags Luke off the second storey deck by his big toe?" Well, we didn't think that would happen and rather figured this idea was pretty clever and would result in a 'Bear roast' in the oven and 'Beargers' in the freezer!)

The first night of bear-hunting season arrived. Our sleeping bags were all set up, my rifle was loaded, the string was firmly tied to the handle of the fruit bucket with the other end to Luke's big toe. We were pretty excited as we turned on the yard light and switched off the deck light. It was late! Luke and I whispered for about 20 minutes in our beds, and then fell asleep with visions of bear rugs dancing in our heads.

Although it seemed like only a few minutes, we were both awakened... by... warm sunshine on our faces. IT WAS MORNING!! We had slept all night without being wakened by the ferocious beast and we assumed that he simply had not come to our yard that night. We both got up and peered over the deck railing into the yard to indeed see... an empty, knocked-over bucket lying in the yard! Aaaarrgghh.... we missed our chance!! Back to the drawing board!

After explaining to all the people in town that we had missed our opportunity, I devised a new and foolproof plan. I would simply sit out on the deck all night with the loaded rifle and quietly wait for the bear to show up. Evening approached, and I moved our recliner chair out onto the deck so that I would have a comfortable place to sit and a perfect line of sight to the back yard. Sandi and our boys, wanting to make sure I would not fall asleep, brought out a big jug of iced tea and a large bowl of popcorn for me. Around 7:00 pm I began waiting out on the deck, it was dark. I watched for four hours... nothing!

At approximately 11:00 pm, Sandi and our boys came out on the deck to say goodnight to me before they went to bed. Just before they came out however, I heard what sounded like a twig snapping just down the mountain trail that leads to our property.

"Shhhh," I said, and told them to be quiet, to just crouch down and wait and watch with me. Several minutes later, from behind one of our fruit trees, we could all see the shadowy figure of the black bear swaggering into the outer limits of our yard light. Slowly but confidently he made his way to the fruit bucket, knocked it over and began to devour his nightly treat. We held our breath in nervous excitement. I lifted the rifle to my shoulder, lined up the bear in the scope and carefully removed the safety by fully cocking the hammer into firing position. The mild 'click' of the hammer being cocked drew the attention of the bear and he stopped eating. He looked up to the source of the sound. I now had the cross hairs of the scope fixed directly between his eyes as he looked right at me, fully illuminated by the yard light. The loud crack of the rifle reverberated off the cliffs and canyons of the surrounding mountains. The bear dropped to the ground, dead at the very moment of the shot. In excitement, victory, and relief, we hooted, hugged and high fived each other while the phone began to ring, and cars arrived in our driveway. People all around our area had been waiting for the resounding shot that would end this small-town crisis. It was the biggest news story in months. Our neighbor lady from next door showed up with her dog and gave me a big 'bear hug' of thanks.

After field dressing the bear, caping out the hide and hanging the carcass, we said goodnight to all our friends and neighbours, and got to bed around 3:00 in the morning, satisfied and relieved to have completed our quest. The bear was cut, wrapped and filled our freezer, supplying roasts, steaks, chops and 'Bearger' for the winter ahead. The hide was tanned and made into a bear rug which hangs on the wall of my brother's cabin at the lake to this day.

In life, sometimes crises and challenges happen, and we have to figure out how to respond. Sometimes our best efforts are unrewarded and instead of just giving up, we have to persevere and try again and again to solve the problems and find a solution. In Heb. 10: 35-36 it says: "So do not throw away your confidence; it will be richly rewarded. You need to persevere so that when you have done the will of God, you will receive what He has promised." (Ask your mom and dad what 'perseverance' is and ask God to help form it as part of your character.)

Prayer: *Lord Jesus, thanks for the challenges that come our way, and help us not to just give up, but to keep seeking You for the answers and solutions that we need. Amen.*

BE SURE YOUR SINS WILL FIND YOU OUT

Earning a driver's license is one of the key events in a young teen's life! It was no different in the 1960's, but neither were there any seat belts, head rests, GPS, computer screens or cruise control. The driver simply sat behind the wheel and navigated the vehicle to its destination in any way that made sense at the time.

I was just a kid and my oldest brother Merl was of driving age. Dad would be driving while we were on a family vacation and Merl would be sitting directly behind him in the back seat. When Dad got tired and needed a break it was considered wasteful to actually pull over and stop to switch drivers, because it would cost both time and fuel to do so. It made the most sense to my dad to switch drivers while we were travelling down the highway at 60 miles per hour (this was before Canada adopted the metric system for distance and speed). Dad would ask Merl to get ready to make the switch from the back seat. Dad would place his left foot on the gas pedal to keep the car speeding down the highway while he 'skootched' over into the middle of the front seat, still steering the car straight with his left hand. Merl, from the back seat, would sling one leg over the back of the front seat and stand on the driver seat while bringing his other leg and body over the bench seat. That done, he could slide down into the driver position behind the wheel and replace dad's foot and hand on the gas pedal and steering wheel. I saw this maneuver many times either by switching to a driver from the back seat or by trading drivers with the middle person on the front bench seat. In this case, Dad lifted up his bum so that the person beside him could slide under him to take the driver position while Dad would squirm to his right into the middle passenger spot.

To avoid having to stop at a gas station when one of us boys needed to use a bathroom, mom and dad decided to bring a large apple juice can into the car and mom would then hand us the can to pee in from the back seat. We would pass the full can back to mom who would carefully hold it on the front floor mat between her feet until we slowed down to pass through a town at 30 mph. When she could safely open the car door a crack, she would pour the foul liquid on the road as we drove through town.

From the age of 11 or 12, we would be allowed to sit on Dad's knee and steer while he operated the gas and brake pedals. All these experiences formed my standards for travelling in a car and made me look forward to the time when I would be in charge of operating a motor vehicle of my own.

At 14 I wrote the Beginner's test and got my Learners license; at 16, with eager anticipation, I booked an appointment to take the driver's test. I still remember the examiner getting into the passenger seat beside me with his clip board and pen, and telling me to pull out of the parking lot and drive down the street. I had practiced with my dad and knew how to parallel park, when to slow down and stop before a traffic light or cross walk, and how to keep both hands on the steering wheel at the 10:00 and 2:00 o'clock positions! I was pretty nervous though when the stone-faced examiner sat next to me and gave gruff instructions on where to go. I also felt a bit distracted while driving down busy Edmonton streets during rush hour traffic. When he told me to turn right at a corner, I got confused and turned left instead. This may not have been a big deal except that I had turned onto a one-way street going the WRONG WAY!! Heavy traffic headed directly toward me and horns honked loudly as vehicles swerved to miss my car. While tightly gripping the steering wheel, I could see the examiner from the corner of my eye shaking his head from side to side with his eyes down and his hand over his forehead. Needless to say, I flunked that driving test, had to practice some more, and booked another exam a couple of weeks later. I finally earned my driver's license, and at the old age of 16, discovered that the thrill of driving was the apex of maturity and personal freedom.

I remember one time when my parents were on vacation for a couple of weeks and had left very clear instructions that I was not to drive the car while they were away. Since I was old enough at the time to stay home by myself, I found the temptation to drive the car on my own almost unbearable, but managed to obey their directions . . . until the day before they arrived home. Who would ever know if I drove the car to school on that last day? What harm could it do? Besides, I had many friends who drove cars to school, so why not me... just this once? I did feel a pang of guilt while sliding behind the wheel, but pride and excitement won out as I pulled out of the garage and confidently cruised to the High School parking lot. I felt so grown up and mature driving Dad's 1968 shiny, blue Pontiac.

I walked toward the building to attend class, but just before rounding the corner I glanced back at the car, proudly noting it was perfectly parked next to other student's cars. I looked forward to having my friends see me walk to the car after school, drive out of the parking lot and down the street. I knew many of them wished their parents would allow them the same freedom.

When the last bell rang, I slowly made my way to the front doors of the school, waiting a bit until all my friends were out of their classes as well, just so they would be outside to see me drive away. Strangely, I had an unmistakable feeling of guilt and foreboding and considered the possibility that something had happened to the car while I had been in classes.

"Ridiculous!" I thought. "What could possibly have happened to the car while it sat in the parking lot? Must just be a bit of excitement that I'm feeling... not guilt or dread."

I rounded the corner of the school building, headed for the parking lot, looked toward where I had parked Dad's car, and saw what looked like damage to the car! As I got closer, I saw that someone had indeed backed into the car and totally caved in the right rear quarter panel! I couldn't believe what I was seeing! How could this possibly have happened? It was in a PARKING LOT for goodness sake! I hadn't even been driving the car and still it had been severely damaged! What would my dad say? What would happen to me? How could I ever explain the damage since I had been clearly told not to drive while my folks were gone! Aaaarrggghhhhhh! I am so toast! I drove the car home and parked in the garage, my mind numb with the horrible thoughts of what awaited me when mom and dad got home. They would arrive the next day. I didn't even have the option of taking the car to an auto body shop to get it fixed before they got home. Guilt and dread were not my friends through that evening and night. They hovered like a heavy, dark blanket over my existence.

The next day my parents arrived. I welcomed them home, fearfully confessed what I had done, and asked them to please forgive me for my foolish disobedience. I was astonished that

Dad did not become angry, yell, or find some creative way to punish me. By my down-turned eyes, shaky voice and defeated body language, he could see how upset I was and recognized my sense of guilt and repentance for such a foolish act of disobedience! He told me he would take the car into an auto body repair shop to get it fixed, but that I would have to work to earn the money to pay for the entire repair bill. Relieved, I willingly did as he asked and never disobeyed him with his car again.

I also asked God to forgive me for my disobedience. I knew that He had known and watched me throughout the entire episode, from the very beginning when I convinced myself that this was a smart thing to do, right to the end when I was guilty and ashamed.

The Bible says to 'Honor your Father and Mother in everything for this is right!' Eph. 6:2 Even though the repair to the fender of the car was not terribly expensive, though it certainly seemed so at the time, it provided me with valuable lessons I will never forget. I learned about obedience, about the sad result of giving into temptation, about honoring parents, about the dangers of pride and rebellion, and about living life under God's watchful and loving eyes. I also learned that confessing my sins and rebellion to God and to those I have hurt, are part of what it takes to experience healing and restored relationships.

Prayer: *Dear Jesus, thank You for using our failures and disobedience to teach us lessons that we need to learn, and for forgiving us no matter what we have done when we come to You in humility and repentance. Amen.*

163

MY DREAM CAR

It was a thing of beauty! I had seen these new sports cars on the road about a year earlier and wondered if I would ever be able to afford one for myself? I was only 16 years old at the time and had recently gotten my driver's license but, as a grade 12 student, buying a car like that seemed impossible or at least far off in the distant future.

Following graduation from high school at the age of 17, I immediately got a job driving forklift at a truss factory. The trusses we made were wooden support structures used for building floors and roof systems in mobile homes. With a paycheque coming in every two weeks, and few other expenses because I was living at home with my folks, I felt rich enough to invest in a vehicle. A car would allow me to drive to work, to church, to take girls out on dates, and generally begin my adult life of independence.

I remember wondering how much those sports cars I had seen a year earlier cost and if it might be possible for me to get one. I asked my dad to come with me to the Toyota car dealership to check out their new sports model called the Toyota Celica. We pulled up to the show room and I saw it! Sitting right there under the fluorescent lights was the car of my dreams. What a car! The one in the show room was fire-engine red and it sparkled and glistened under the lights. The pure-white upholstery and elaborate dash board seemed like a fighter plane cockpit to me. I slid behind the wheel, grasped the steering wheel with my left hand, the stick shift knob with my right, and could almost hear the smooth roar of the engine as I imagined speeding down the highway, passing every other vehicle on the road.

The price tag was $3700.00 the salesman told us, in cash, or by monthly payments of $225 for 2 years. Wow, $225 per month . . . that was almost half of what I earned each month! I discussed it with my dad who, although he felt $225 a month was far too much for a 17-year-old kid to commit to, wanted me to learn by making my own decision.

"Does the car come in turquoise blue?" I asked the salesman.

"It does," he replied with a smile, "but it will have to be

ordered in and would take about two weeks."

I was hooked! I signed the sales contract and paid the down payment to secure the deal, with my dad co-signing to confirm the sale. The next weeks were the longest two weeks of my life as I waited for that beautiful car to be delivered. Finally, on Nov 30, 1973, my turquoise Toyota Celica arrived and Dad went with me to the car dealership to pick it up. What a beautiful sight! The car was sitting out in front of the main showroom doors boasting "I belong to Del Riemer! Everyone take a look and eat your hearts out!" Once the final papers were signed, the keys were in my hand, and the licence plate screwed into place, Dad and I got into the car for the ride home. Because I didn't know how to drive a standard stick shift yet, my dad drove the car home while I sat in the passenger seat and marveled at the amazing sports car that was now mine! On the drive home through the heart of town, I noticed every person who glanced at the car and excitedly imagined they were all jealous. When we arrived, Dad pulled his big family car out of the garage and parked the Celica in its place for safe keeping.

My 18th birthday was still three weeks away. To get the best rate of insurance on the car, I needed to wait until I turned 18 and that meant I couldn't drive the car at all for three weeks! Each night after work I would sit in the car, listen to the radio, start the engine, and very carefully pull ahead in the garage a foot or two, and then back up a foot or two, just to practice driving. I even decided to customize the car a bit while it sat there in the garage. I brought out my white model paints, and carefully painted the letters on the tires white so they would stand out for when I would finally be able to drive the car. I installed two wedge speaker boxes in the back window so that the sound of the car stereo would be louder and more 'bassy'. To customize the car further, I cut a piece of gold, two-inch shag rug and fit it into the back window which was the 'cool' thing to do back then. Lastly, I added two 'fog lights' to the front bumper which made the car look tougher, faster and much 'cooler' than any other Celica on the road. I knew the car was brand new but I couldn't help polishing it every day. I even got out my dad's 'Turtle Wax', and applied a coat of wax, buffing it to a sparkling, shiny finish. As those 21 days slowly ticked by, my excitement and anticipation grew to a fever pitch and I scratched off each date on the calendar up until December 21, 1973 when I would turn 18 years old! Have you ever been sooooo excited that you could hardly stand it? That's how I felt!

The day finally came when I could buy my car insurance, put the sticker on the license plate and take my beautiful turquoise sports car out of the garage and drive it down the road. Since I still needed to learn how to drive the standard transmission smoothly, the first couple of days were not very impressive as the car jerked forward when I let out the clutch too quickly. My inexperience caused the car to stall several times as I tried to go forward when a traffic light turned green, but I finally got the hang of it and soon I was smoothly driving down the road with my radio turned up and the fog lights turned on.

Many of my friends and co-workers were jealous of my fancy new car, and I kind of liked it that way! I kept it sparkling clean and offered rides to anyone I knew who needed a lift. Over the course of that year I began to realize that this car was my prized possession, and that my pride was getting unhealthy. When I prayed or talked about how much I loved Jesus, I knew in my heart that if I was honest, I'd have to admit that I loved my car even more! I wanted people to notice me driving down the street and I loved it when they asked me about the car and how much I had paid for it. I guess it made me feel superior and successful. I knew that my car was becoming way too important in my life, and I also knew that I needed to do something about it, but when you love something so much, it's hard to let go. I came to the place with my sports car where I knew I had to give it up. I put it up for sale and sold it to a friend of mine who had admired it ever since I had bought it. It's a funny thing, but after I sold that car, I felt better! I knew there were things that were more important to me than 'stuff'!

Sometimes in life, we think 'things' will make us happy. We want something so bad that everything else fades behind our desire for that 'One Thing'! Other people, caring for one another, being obedient, working hard and simple kindness, all get forgotten as we just wallow in the pleasure of 'that one thing'. God reminds us that we need to seek Him first, and then all the rest will fall into place.

Prayer: *Lord, thank You for continuing to remind us of what is truly important, and being patient with us even when we put our attention on the wrong things. Keep our hearts seeking after the things that will last and the ways we can bring You pleasure. Amen.*

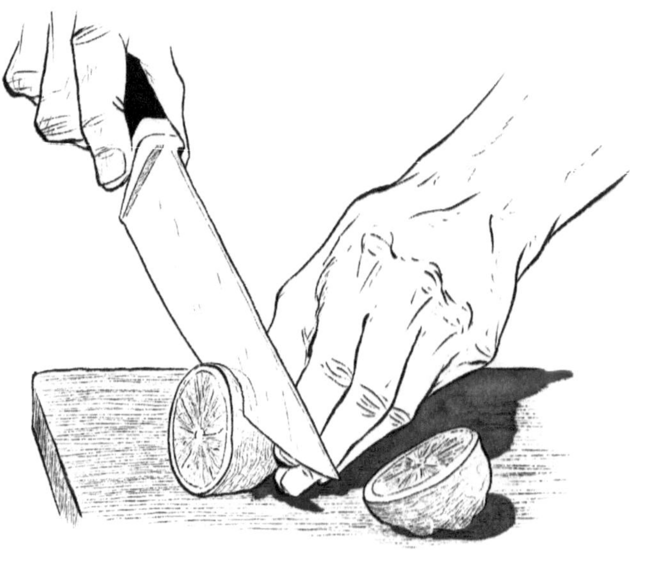

THE LEMON

Everyone should work at a restaurant at some point in their lives! I know that for me it was a great way to learn some important people skills. A job at McDonalds or any fast food restaurant is also a good way for young people to develop a strong work ethic. My experience was with The Keg back in the late 1970's. I had just come off a four-year road tour with one of the early Gospel Rock 'n Roll bands and I needed work. A friend got me an interview at the Abbotsford Keg restaurant and I was hired as a busboy and dishwasher. Although I was 21 years old, and it wasn't my first job, this seemed like a whole new adventure. My dad had taught me that when you work for someone else, you should look them straight in the eye, shake their hand firmly, and show respect for them by working hard. You come into work a bit early, do whatever is asked, and you stay a bit later than the rest of the employees, showing that you are responsible, trust-worthy and eager. Dad called this a work ethic, or simply what it takes to keep a job and move up in responsibility and pay scale.

Working at the Keg, I would go in early to get the back end of the restaurant ready for opening. I folded the cloth napkins, made up extra place settings, got the dishwashing area organized and made a point of getting to know the other employees. I enjoyed the work and was quickly given more responsibility. Before long, I was promoted to 'waiter', and was eventually offered the chance to train for a management position. This was an honor, but it also meant that before becoming a full manager, I had to first learn every job in the restaurant. Besides serving customers, I had to learn how to bartend, prep in the kitchen, and cook all the meals on the menu. I also had to order all the food and restaurant supplies, train staff, make up employee schedules, record all the money that was taken in and pay all the bills. I loved every part of the restaurant business, and, since I was now newly married, I could make enough money to start a family and even buy a house! I managed the Abbotsford Keg restaurant and then later took over the Coquitlam Keg as the General Manager.

One busy Saturday night when the restaurant was full of customers and with a lineup at the door, I was sitting in my office working on the financial ledger when Randy, one of our head cooks, knocked on my office door. He seemed a bit uncomfortable as he told me there was a pretty angry customer who wanted to speak with me.

"Do you know what the problem is, Randy?" I asked.

"Ummm, well, we were fooling around in the broiler bar and I threw a lemon at one of the other cooks, just for fun. The cook ducked and the lemon flew over his head into the restaurant and hit a customer at table #15 in the head," Randy replied, appearing embarrassed and sheepish. (The broiler bar was where the food was prepared for the customers and was in an area visible to the whole restaurant.) Randy admitted that the man at that table was pretty mad and wanted to speak to the manager.

"I'm really sorry, Del," Randy said. With a deep sigh, I knew I would have to talk with the angry customers and try to calm things down.

After composing myself, and telling Randy to go back to work, I carefully made my way out to Table #15 where an elderly lady was sitting across from her son and his wife. I could tell right away they were unhappy customers and were just waiting to tell me how their evening had been ruined. I approached their table, and introduced myself as the manager.

"I understand there has been an incident here at your table," I said.

The man spoke angrily so I squatted down to his level to hear his story. I couldn't help but notice the elderly lady's hair was matted down, and that she had traces of sour cream and butter matted in her hair, on one ear, and hanging out of one nostril. The son was very upset. "We came into your restaurant to celebrate our 25th wedding anniversary with my mother, fully expecting we could count on a nice evening with good service and a quality meal! Then a lemon, thrown by one of your staff members, came flying out of the kitchen and knocked my mother in the back of her head with such force that her head jerked down, plastering her face into her meal." The man was clearly disturbed.

"We are so upset we will never come back to this restaurant again! I hope you fire your employee as payment from us. Our evening has been ruined!" he continued.

As I squatted attentively by the table, I listened carefully to what the man was saying. When he was done, I truly felt bad for them and the way our thoughtless staff had ruined an otherwise happy celebration.

"If I was in your situation and came here to have a nice evening celebration with my dear mother, and then had such a terrible and careless thing happen, I would feel exactly the same way as you do. I wouldn't blame you at all if you decided to never come back here again and you told your friends what a horrible evening you have had. Frankly, we deserve it!" The visibly upset customers nodded in agreement. I continued,

"I know I can't change what has happened here tonight, and I will certainly deal with the staff member who caused this, but I want you to know that it is definitely not what we stand for in this restaurant. I can assure you that this will never happen again. In order to at least salvage some small part of your evening, I will not be charging you anything for your meal tonight and I would like to offer you each a dessert and special after-dinner coffee following your meal. In addition, I would like to give you a gift certificate covering the full cost of your next meal here at the Keg, if you would consider giving us a chance to make up for this unfortunate experience. Please, enjoy the rest of your meal, and I will come back personally to take your dessert order when you are ready." The couple and their mother seemed pleasantly surprised with my offer. I suppose they were expecting that I would just apologize, and offer to pay for a portion of their meal, but my attitude, along with the offer of another free meal as well as my personal service, seemed to have taken the sting and anger out of their frustration and irritation.

After bringing over a clean, damp cloth to wipe up their table (and another to allow their mother to 'touch up',) I allowed time for them to finish their meal before returning to clear dishes and take their dessert and drink order.

I soon returned and placed extra-large portions of dessert in front of them and asked them about their 25 years together, how they had met and what had been the highlight of their marriage? Before long, they invited me to sit down next to 'Mom' to chat. We spoke about our families and careers, and they even wanted to know what it was like for me to run a large restaurant. We spent maybe 15 or 20 minutes talking and laughing before they rose to leave. Before the three of them left the table, we shook hands and I gave them the promised gift certificate for their next meal, thanked them for the great conversation and for being so understanding about the situation with the lemon.

After the restaurant had closed for the night and the kitchen had been cleaned up, I asked Randy to come into my office for a chat. He knocked on the door and stepped, somewhat anxiously, into the office with his head down and shoulders slumped.

"Randy," I said sternly, "you have always been a valued and reliable team member here, I can hardly believe you would do such a stupid thing as you did tonight. To salvage the evening celebration for that couple and his mom, I had to give them almost $200 in meals and gift certificates. If you ever, pull anything like that again, I will fire you on the spot. Do you know what the worst part of all this was?" Randy, with his eyes to the floor quietly remained standing. "What?" he asked.

"Well, when I first went to their table and listened to their angry voices, I couldn't help but notice the glob of sour cream hanging out of the old lady's nose. It was very hard not to crack up laughing!" I looked straight at Randy with an understanding smile. He lifted his head, almost in disbelief that I was not angry with him anymore and was actually making light of the situation. He laughed rather nervously as I spoke again: "Time to go home now. Don't forget about tonight, but don't worry about it either. You're a good guy Randy!" Then he left.

That couple not only came back for their free meal, but they became regular customers, coming at least once a week for the next year or so. We actually became friends and I would often sit and chat with them. Over time, Randy became our head broiler chef and was one of our best staff members for several years.

This restaurant management experience taught two important lessons: First, when there is a problem, we need to treat people kindly and with respect, and try to make things right. Sometimes, things will turn out even better than expected. The customers came back often, and I made new friends as well! Second, everyone makes mistakes and we do foolish things sometimes, like Randy did, but it is generally wise to give people a second chance and allow them to learn from their mistakes. God has been gracious to me over the years, especially considering all the mistakes I have made, but He continues to love me and doesn't give up on me. He will certainly never give up on you either!

Prayer: *Lord Jesus, thanks for never giving up on us and loving us no matter what. Help us to see other people the way You see them and let us be quick to forgive. Amen.*

SHELL
SHELL
HELL
HELL

CHAPTER 22

BEETLE BOARD

In a previous story, I mentioned my beautiful turquoise Toyota Celica sports car which I had become obsessed with, and it became the cause of unhealthy personal pride and arrogance. Because of those attitudes I had felt the need to sell the car and buy something simpler, cheaper and less flashy. After a little searching, I found a light blue, beat up, 1968 Volkswagen Beetle for $800. It had a few dents in the body, a cracked windshield, and a couple of small rips in the seats, but it was just what I needed. Although it was not pretty to look at, the Beetle was a reliable and fun car to drive. In the winter time there was a bit of a problem because the windshield would get all frosted up on both the outside and on the inside. With no defroster in the car I had to scrape the outside of the windshield, and then do the inside as well, with all the frosty ice scrapings falling down on the dash and the seats. The car was not equipped with either a heater or a fan and the windshield would keep frosting up and needing to be scraped even while I was driving. What a pain that was!

Summer came. I considered fixing the dents, getting rid of some rust and making the car look a bit nicer, but I just didn't have the money. One day, while reading the Edmonton Journal newspaper, I saw an advertisement for 'Beetle Boards'. A company was looking for anyone who owned a Volkswagen Beetle to apply at their office to have their car transformed into a mobile billboard for advertising purposes. Curious, I drove my bug to their office and completed an application. A few days later, I received a phone call telling me that my car had been accepted as a 'Beetle Board', and that I should bring it to their body shop the next morning to begin the transformation.

When I arrived at the shop, the manager asked me which company I would prefer to advertise for, A&W or GWG Jeans. If I chose A&W, they would do all the body work on the car, paint it white, and a large mural of the A&W Root Bear would be painted on the front hood. On the back of the car it would say: "Follow me to A&W."

I thought that would be pretty cool, but I asked what the GWG Beetle Board would look like. He told me that they would again do all the body work, fix the rust, put in a new windshield, and paint the car to look like a pair of jeans, complete with the denim color, yellow stitching around the windows, back pockets and a zipper. On the roof just above the side windows would be printed: "Gee but I love my GWG's." 'Wow,' I thought, 'I could be driving a car that looks like a pair of jeans... I'll take it!'

The body work and custom paint job took about ten days to complete. The phone call finally came. My 'Beetle Board' was ready. I got a ride down to the body shop and, with excitement, rounded the corner of the parking lot to see an amazing sight. My car was sitting in front of the big shop doors, gleaming in the sunlight. The entire car looked just like denim with yellow stitching around every window and door. On the rear of the car were two back pockets bordered in yellow stitching and the main feature was a huge metal flake zipper running straight up the hood with the pull tab just below the windshield. "Gee but I love my GWG's" was printed above the windows, as promised.

I was stunned! I was attending college at the time and I could hardly wait to drive my new 'Beetle Board' to school and take my roommate and friends for a drive! Before leaving the body shop, I had to sign some papers and only then did I learn that along with getting my car 'transformed' free of charge, I would also get a free pair of GWG jeans every month, to keep or to give away, to friends or family. What a deal!

When I drove into the college dorm parking lot, I was swarmed by students gawking at my car, taking pictures, and asking to go for a cruise. Since this was back in 1975, and seatbelts were not yet mandatory, I took the back seat out and crammed nine people into the car. We drove to Dairy Queen and with ice cream cones for everyone, cruised the streets of Edmonton for a couple of hours.

Transformation is an amazing thing. My car was a cheap, old, beat-up Volkswagen that no one would have paid any attention to, but once it was cleaned up, repainted and decorated, it took on a whole new life. I am reminded that God accepts us just as we are, with all our weaknesses, dents and struggles. He works on us day by day to make us into people who reflect His character and draw others to Him. The Bible says: "Therefore, if any man is in Christ, he is a new creation; the old things are passed away; behold, all things are become new." II Cor. 5:17

Prayer: *Dear Jesus, thanks for being willing to accept me as I am and making me into a new creation because of Your life in me. Amen.*

BIRDS IN THE CHIMNEY

A couple of years before Sandi, my wife, became ill and consequently permanently disabled, we lived on Thetis Island in a small house right on the ocean front with stunning views of eagles, sea life, and small islands that dotted the vista from our front porch. Sandi loved to take breaks from running the college book and snack shop by going for walks in the 'back 40' of the school property. There were several miles of beautiful trails that meandered through the lush, rainforest environment. The forest was home to Douglas firs, red cedars, arbutus trees, various moss and ferns, along with deer, small animals and birds. Sandi had a favorite bench where she loved to sit and bask in the warm sunshine, listen to the sounds of the forest, and revel in the stunning panorama of the ocean in the distance. One day she discovered a gnarled, old, burled maple tree which became her 'Enchanted Tree'. Birds would perch, sing and chirp their greetings in the branches of that old tree. Sandi would close her eyes, listen to 'creation' speak, and then would respond with praise and thanksgiving in her heart while communing with her Heavenly Father. This favorite pastime, which gave her so much joy and perspective, was lost when she fell ill. Many things in her life changed after that.

The house we lived in was an older home about a hundred yards from the ocean shore line. It had a beautiful enclosed front porch and a tall brick chimney that, from the foundation, climbed up one side of the house. Over the years the house had settled and the brick and mortar of the fireplace chimney separated slightly from the outside siding of the house creating a small protected space between the house and the chimney. For the first few years we never had an issue with that space, but shortly after Sandi got sick some small birds chose to move in and make it their home.

Come springtime, the birds would flutter into the cavity behind the fireplace, delivering grass, twigs and other materials to build their nest. From inside the house we could often hear their muffled shuffling activity just behind the fireplace bricks, but it was not overly distracting. When the nest was complete, the birds would lay eggs and then the young birds would hatch with newly formed lungs and ravenous appetites. When mom or dad would show up with a juicy worm for their young, the chicks would compete to see who could chirp, squawk or peep the loudest and get the next morsel. The noise of this 'squawkfest' was annoying and began to grate on my nerves, especially during the height of the chick's growth spurt when it seemed like a parent bird would arrive with food every 3 or 4 minutes.

Increasingly aggravated and annoyed, I rationalized that I should be a good steward of the house and close up the space caused by the sinking brick chimney. Some insulation and additional siding would close the opening and fix the defect. More importantly, it would get rid of those pesky birds that were disturbing the peace and tranquility of our home.

On a day off from work, I announced my intention to go and rout out those annoying birds from our chimney and seal off the opening where they had gained access.

"Del, you will do no such thing!" Sandi responded with surprising firmness. "You will leave those birds alone! Before I got sick, I could hike up in the forest trails and enjoy the wind rustling through the leaves of the trees and the wonderful sounds of the birds that congregated there in my enchanted tree. Now that I am no longer able to go there to commune with God and all His marvelous creatures, He is showing His love, by bringing them to me." She continued, "Every time I hear those birds rustling and chirping behind the fireplace bricks, it reminds me that God knows just where I am, and He is faithful and loving, even though I am disabled and confined to this house."

I had no idea Sandi felt that way. I had been totally consumed by my own selfish annoyance and frustration with those pesky intruders. Once Sandi explained her appreciation for how God had acknowledged her need by 'bringing the forest to her', I actually began to look forward to the sounds of those little creatures in our home, almost like welcoming them as guests sent by God Himself.

Sometimes we need to look at our situation from someone else's point of view. Only then can we see what God wants us to see. There is always more than one way to understand things. If we can take some time to watch and listen, we can avoid jumping to conclusions and making decisions that might hurt someone else.

"Consider the birds of the air," Jesus said, "that they do not sow, neither do they reap, nor gather into barns, and yet your heavenly Father feeds them. Are you not worth much more than they?" Matt. 6:26

Prayer: *Jesus, thank You that You know just how to show us that You love us. Give us eyes that see Your activity, especially when we tend to jump to conclusions that might be selfish or hurt someone else. And thanks for showing us clearly Your character through all that You have made. Amen.*

BROMLEY ROCK

My legs felt rubbery and my mind was numb with fear as we stood atop the 72-foot-high, solid-rock pinnacle looking down into the swirling current of the Similkameen River.

Let me explain. Bromley Rock is a Provincial campground and rest stop area on Highway #3, near where we used to live in Hedley, B.C., Canada. During the summer months this area is cluttered with cars, trailers, RV's, and thousands of tourists who vacation through the scenic Southern BC interior. The Bromley Rock tower is located on a bend in the river which, during the spring runoff, deposits a large quantity of sand on the near shore, making an inviting beach on the bank of the Similkameen. Sun bathers, swimmers, and families congregate there to enjoy the cool water of the meandering river and the rare, fine sandy beach in the midst of a rugged mountain pass. Bromley Rock itself rises 72 feet to its highest point. After a short swim across the river from the beach area, a cliff-jumper can follow a rocky trail to several 'jump off' points of varying heights. The lowest ledge is roughly only 10 feet above water level, but the highest point is an intimidating 72 feet. The Rocky outcrops that jut out from the vertical drop-off are added challenges, forcing the jumper to push hard out and away from the rocks.

It was on one hot summer day in July that my two friends, Jim and Jerry, joined me at the beach where there were many other people enjoying the sun, sand and water. Jerry had his video camera and the three of us imagined making an exciting home movie of us jumping off the top of Bromley Rock into the river. We had watched one or two other brave souls navigate the river and the rocky trail to the second highest point on the rock. They jumped into the water to the "oooh's," "aahhh's", and applause of the spectators on the beach. The crowd approval spurred us to climb, foolishly, all the way to the highest perch on the rock to attempt the death-defying leap.

Jerry stayed on the beach to film the epic attempt. Jim and I swam across the river and climbed to the very top of Bromley

Rock. From that vantage point we anxiously surveyed the terrifying drop below with great fear and trepidation. I was a rock-climbing instructor at the time and not afraid of heights . . . . but below us there was a swirling river with a strong current. We would have to leap far out to avoid the jutting, jagged rocks. The intimidation and fear factors were acute. Spectators on the beach yelled up encouragement and spurred us on to make the mighty leap into the river. It was several minutes before we were able to work up enough nerve to jump. Jim and I looked at each other, peered over the edge, looked at each other again, laughed nervously; then we stilled the noise of the onlookers with our outstretched arms. On the beach, Jerry steadied the video camera to record the spectacular feat.

Jim and I shifted our weight back on our feet to create momentum and then, on the count of three, exploded forward, propelling ourselves as far out and away from the rock as possible. We prepared ourselves in midair for the violent collision with the cold, swirling water below. I felt suspended in mid-air for a full minute though it was actually closer to three seconds.

Fortunately, I was still wearing sneakers from the climb up the rock because the soles of my feet slapped the water with great force, and I could feel the jarring concussion in my hips. We both sunk down into the water but the river was deep enough that our feet did not touch bottom. We rose to the surface, high fived each other to the cheers of the beach spectators, then swam back across the river to a hero's welcome. Wow! What an exhilarating experience! We basked in the appreciation of the crowd for a few minutes before crossing the river again and repeating the jump with much more confidence and gusto.

Jerry had been filming our jumps and once we got back to him, we strongly suggested that he go do a jump and we would film it for him. Jerry was not interested in doing such a risky and frightening thing. It took much cajoling, motivating, belittling and manipulating on our part to get him to give it a go! I am embarrassed to say that I, young and foolish, put huge peer pressure on Jerry to make his attempt. Reluctantly, Jerry swam across the river, climbed to the top of Bromley Rock and paced back and forth in that small area, trying to work up the courage to make the leap. Meanwhile, I was filming with his camera and adding an immature and ill-advised commentary, saying things like, "Jerry has so much hair on his chest that he is not very aerodynamic," and "Jerry's nostrils are so big that they will act like two parachutes and slow his decent." After all the encouragement and whistling from the crowd below, Jerry finally took the leap and fell awkwardly into the river current, splashing into the water in a sitting position. I made some foolish comment on the video like, "Incredible, the worlds' first 'bum' dive!"

When Jerry's head finally broke the surface of the water, I could see immediately that something was horribly wrong. His eyes were as big as saucers and he was awkwardly struggling against the current. As he was being swept down-river, I switched off the camera, dove into the water, and swam to him as fast as I could.

"Help me, Del, I can't feel my legs." Jerry sounded really scared. As an Outdoor Mountain Guide with Back Country First Aid training, I knew that the next minutes would be critical to get Jerry immobilized and transferred to a medical care facility. Once I had towed him back to the shoreline, I organized a group of onlookers to support him as I held his head and neck in supportive traction while sending someone for help. This was long before cell phones so someone had to drive the 20 minutes to Princeton, the closest hospital, for help. A screaming ambulance finally arrived, rushed Jerry to Princeton for assessment and from there he was airlifted by helicopter to the Shaughnessy Hospital Spinal Cord Unit in Vancouver. He had suffered three crushed vertebrae, as well as a compressed spinal cord, and was unable to move his legs for over a month. He remained in hospital for several months after surgery, and then underwent rehabilitation for a full year after that.

I visited Jerry in the hospital shortly after the accident and was harshly scolded by his physiotherapist who had heard the full account of what had happened. She knew that I was the one who had manipulated him into taking that fateful and foolish plunge. "Hitting the water from that height is like landing on concrete. To try such a stupid thing, and then to pressure someone else to do it as well is criminal," she said angrily.

I felt, guilty, sad, immature and ashamed for what I had done, and for the harm it had caused. I wondered if Jerry would ever forgive me... especially since he could relive the events over and over whenever he watched it on video. During the visit, Jerry was polite and friendly, but didn't really say much. I interpreted his quietness as anger and not wanting to lash out at me in front of others.

Three years passed without me seeing Jerry again though we talked a few times on the phone. Then, one summer, he asked if he could come to our place for a talk and visit. I was afraid of what he would say and prepared myself for his words.

"Del, I just wanted to tell you not to be too hard on yourself for what happened back at Bromley Rock," he began. "Yes, it was a very tragic accident and many lessons were learned that day, but I am actually grateful that it happened to me." I was stunned. How could such a terrible event have any good come out of it? I listened closely as he continued.

"Before I came out that weekend to spend time with you, I had been living a lie for years. I called myself a Christian, attended church and said 'Christian' things, but in my heart I was just living for myself. I never really talked to God, never considered His desires for my life, and I was engaged in many foolish and self-destructive things. After the accident I had to take a hard look at my life and decide what was really important, like, who could I trust and whether God was really real." Jerry paused for a moment to take a deep breath.

"You know, Del, God showed His love and faithfulness to me, and He became my closest friend. He still is. Because of that accident, I am a different man today, and I'll never go back! Thank you for your friendship, and please, do not beat yourself up. What was perhaps a foolish mistake, God meant for good, and He has turned it into a great blessing in my life." I felt shocked, humbled, relieved, and recognized once again that God is able to use anything in our lives to draw us back to Himself.

I have never forgotten the lessons I learned that day, even though I am still learning more lessons year by year. God is good. God is faithful. God forgives. God can heal deep wounds of body, mind, and spirit, and He will continue to walk with us and transform us if we surrender to Him daily.

Prayer: *Dear Jesus, thank You for using our mistakes to teach us lessons, and for protecting our heart and mind from things that could destroy us. Save us from pride and arrogance which only hurt us and others we love. Use us, God, to encourage each other to do 'good' things that will build us up and draw us to You. Amen.*

THE MAGPIE

When I came home from the office for lunch, I went around to the back of our new house which we were still finishing, and found our siding contractor, Clark, standing on the back lawn looking up at the back side of our house, in tears. Seemed a bit strange to see a burly tradesman broken and in tears, so I asked him if I could help in any way. Clark told me a story which reinforced my understanding and admiration for the great God we serve.

He started his story which seemed very far removed from anything to do with his work on our house. Clark is a passionate follower of Jesus, and he attends a church which is steeped in legalism. (Legalism is just a term that describes people who believe that the main way to follow God is to obey the rules.) Clark understood that God desires His children to live in freedom and rest; to simply allow the goodness and grace of God to be lived out through our lives, rather than obeying rules and doing so with an attitude of criticism, guilt and pride. Clark occasionally preached and taught Sunday School emphasizing these principles. His church did not take kindly to his message of grace, freedom and rest found in Christ, and so they banned him from preaching or teaching. This church felt that their brand of Christianity was under threat by his teaching and that their children were not safe to hear the message he was so passionate about. Clark was devastated and discouraged, wondering what God was doing and what he should do. While deep in thought about this issue, Clark was working on the scaffolding he had built to allow him to apply siding, right up to the peak of our house. He was working about ten feet down from the very top of our house while standing on a 12-inch-wide plank, secured at both ends. While he worked, he noticed a Magpie perched up on the very peak of our house, quietly watching him work. Magpies are generally skittish and noisy birds that will fly away whenever something comes near them. They squawk and jeer noisily at anything or anyone that they think is a threat to them. This Magpie, however, just sat there quietly and watched Clark work, not twelve feet away. Clark was curious about the bird and stopped working to watch it. After a minute or two, the bird hopped down onto the same plank Clark was standing on and fixed its eyes on Clark. Amazed, Clark stood motionless with his tape measure partially extended. As he watched, the bird flew up from the plank and landed on the end of Clark's tape measure which was extended only about twelve inches. The inquisitive bird looked straight into his eyes. Clark told me that both he and the bird stayed in that position for maybe two minutes as they watched each other intently. Clark's eyes began to tear up as he finally sensed what God, his creator, was trying to communicate to him.

When I found Clark in the back yard sobbing, he explained to me that God had just spoken to him up on that scaffolding through that strange and amazing magpie. The bird was not afraid of him but seemed confident and at peace being in the near presence of a human being. He said that it was as if God was saying: "Clark, you are my messenger, and no one should be afraid of what you are teaching because you are simply passing on what I have given you to say. You are loved, and I want to use you as my servant to pass on my love, forgiveness and faithfulness to people who are trying to earn my favour rather than just accepting it as a free gift. Don't stop Clark, don't stop! I am with you!"

I have seen many Magpies over the years but never have I heard of one who has done what this little bird did. I believe that God used that bird to communicate something to Clark that no one else could communicate. It was simply one of God's creatures obeying its creator. I think this is a lesson we can all learn. God desires that we listen, hear his voice and obey, allowing Him to use our voice, hands, feet and attitude to share His heart of love and truth with people we encounter.

Later that summer I was working on my back deck finishing the hand rails and some final siding when a Magpie sat nearby and watched me work. It reminded me once again of the importance of allowing the life of Christ, which lives in every believer, to use us however He desires, to show love and truth to all those we meet.

Prayer: *Lord Jesus, thank You for being able to use us to share Your love with other people. Help me to listen and be obedient to you just like that Magpie did. And God, let me know the freedom, grace and rest You provide for me each day. Amen.*

9 781777 149109